GRUBER'S
ESSENTIAL GUIDE
TO TEST TAKING:
GRADES 3-5

D1212349

<u>Also Available from Gary Gruber and Skyhorse Publishing</u>

Gruber's Complete SAT Guide 2019-2020
Gruber's Complete ACT Guide 2019-2020
Gruber's Complete GRE Guide 2019-2020
Gruber's Essential Guide to Test Taking: Grades 6-9
Gruber's Word Master for Standardized Tests

More information is available at www.drgarygruber.com
and www.skyhorsepublishing.com

GRUBER'S
ESSENTIAL GUIDE
TO TEST TAKING:
GRADES 3-5

The Best Strategies for the Best Score

GARY R. GRUBER, PhD

Skyhorse Publishing
New York, NY

Copyright © 2019 by Gary R. Gruber

All Rights Reserved. No part of this book may be reproduced in any manner without the express written consent of the publisher, except in the case of brief excerpts in critical reviews or articles. All inquiries should be addressed to Skyhorse Publishing, 306 West 37th Street, 11th Floor, New York, NY 10018.

All brand names and product names used in this book are trademarks, registered trademarks, or trade names of their respective holders. Skyhorse Publishing is not associated with any product or vendor in this book.

Skyhorse Publishing books may be purchased in bulk at special discounts for sales promotion, corporate gifts, fund-raising, or educational purposes. Special editions can also be created to specifications. For details, contact the Special Sales Department, Skyhorse Publishing, 306 West 37th Street, 11th Floor, New York, NY 10018 or info@skyhorsepublishing.com.

Skyhorse® and Skyhorse Publishing® are registered trademarks of Skyhorse Publishing, Inc.®, a Delaware corporation.

Visit our website at www.skyhorsepublishing.com.

10 9 8 7 6 5 4 3 2 1

Library of Congress Cataloging-in-Publication Data is available on file.

Cover design by Daniel Brount

Print ISBN: 978-1-5107-5426-3
Ebook ISBN: 978-1-5107-5427-0

Printed in the United States of America

Dedicated to the memory of my parents, Edward and Martha, who gave me the interest, encouragement, and support for my lifelong mission, and to my treasured wife, Raquel, who continues that support and encouragement.

And dedicated to parents and teachers who want to see their children reach their greatest potential, develop a passion for learning, and excel in school and in life.

Acknowledgments

I am grateful to the many parents and teachers who kept prodding me to write this book, and to those parents and teachers who reviewed the work.

I would like to thank my own parents, whose inspiration and concern when I was a child stimulated and nurtured my intense interest in helping parents and teachers get their children to reach their highest potential in school and in life.

CONTENTS

MATH STRATEGIES

INTRODUCTION TO PARENTS

As a parent, you are the *only* person who can guide your child through the trauma of the test-taking experience. With the strategies and methods presented in this book—with which you yourself will be fascinated—you can help your child to realize his or her true potential and to score what he or she should be scoring on all standardized tests. The earlier your child learns these methods, the more they will become second nature to him or her and the more your child will be able to use them on upcoming tests and in schoolwork. This book will increase dramatically your child's critical-thinking ability and test-wiseness. *It is probably the most important book you can read and share with your child for your child's future.*

This book has developed out of the thousands of hours I have spent teaching parents to help their children avoid the emotional shocks resulting from low test scores, and from seemingly poor learning potential and low confidence—shocks that can cause substantial and lasting damage to the psychological and educational development of the child. The methods presented in this book are so universal that by the time your child takes a Scholastic Aptitude Test (SAT), he or she probably won't even have to prepare for it!

When I was eleven years old, I scored 90 on my first IQ test, which was far below average. Had it not been for my father, who questioned the low score, and my own eventual development of strategies for thinking and test taking, I would never have become what I am today—"the nation's leading authority on test taking and author of thirty books on the subject."

As a parent, you must, likewise, prevent the destructive frustration that your child may experience as a result of not knowing how to reach his or her true potential. Nip that frustration in the bud by showing your child the way to demonstrate his or her true smartness, which every child has.

Here's an example of a question that appears on many intelligence tests and on most other standardized tests. Knowing the correct strategy for answering such questions can make the difference of 30 points in an IQ, determine whether or not your child gets into a private school, and whether or not he or she learns how to think correctly.

Is Column A greater than, less than, or equal to Column B?

Column A	Column B
$7 \times 9 \times 4$	$4 \times 7 \times 8$

If your child multiplies the numbers in Column A and in Column B and then compares them, he or she will take too long and not have time to answer many other questions, or, perhaps, will make a mistake. The thinking strategy is to realize that calculating the products in the columns is *not* the simplest thing to do to solve the problem. And you always want your child to take the simplest approach.

Your child simply has to *cancel common numbers* from both columns, as follows:

<table>
<tr><td><u>**Column A**</u></td><td></td><td><u>**Column B**</u></td></tr>
<tr><td>$\not{7} \times 9 \times \not{4}$</td><td></td><td>$\not{4} \times \not{7} \times 8$</td></tr>
</table>

And is left with:

<table>
<tr><td><u>**Column A**</u></td><td></td><td><u>**Column B**</u></td></tr>
<tr><td>9</td><td></td><td>8</td></tr>
</table>

The obvious answer is that Column A is greater than Column B.

Who knows? If your child masters this and many other such strategies and thinking skills, he or she may become a great mathematician. At least your child will like math and do better on tests. And the same holds true for verbal areas.

A Word About the Psychology of Working with Your Child

Much of the material presented in this book will be as fascinating to you as it will be to your child. However, it is important that your child gradually internalize the methods and techniques and not just memorize them. So you have to work patiently with your child and slowly in some cases.

What you want to do is to gradually build your child's confidence by giving your child the tools and methods presented in this book. But don't rush it—go at the pace of your child. Even if your child grasps only a portion of what's in this book, he or she will be far ahead and make significant progress in school and on tests. This book should get you and your child to truly share an exciting learning experience together. However, it is possible, in some cases, that because of your particular interaction with your child, it may be wiser for you to get someone else (an objective non-family member) to work with your child. You can find the names of such people by contacting your child's school principal or counselor. In any event, I cannot stress how important it is, if you do work with your child, for you to be patient and share your child's excitement at his or her own pace. You will find that you and your child will obtain a truly rewarding, multifaceted experience.

The main purpose of this book is to show you how to help your child to take a test without fear, and how to develop your child's true potential.

This book describes for you, in clear-cut language, the various strategies and critical-thinking skills that your child should know for each of the types of questions found on standardized tests. You will quickly see how effective these strategies are, and you will learn how to answer questions using them. You should demonstrate for your child each strategy presented in this book by working with him or her on the sample questions and explanations given in the Strategy sections. Then, after going over the sample questions, you should have your child work on the additional questions at the end of each Strategy section. You will want to go over these questions carefully with your child to see whether he or she has solved them in the same strategic way that was demonstrated in this book.

In summary: Here's the most effective plan for teaching your child the strategies found in this book.

STEP 1. PARENT: Read and understand the strategies and examples given in each of the Strategy sections in this book.

STEP 2. PARENT: Explain to your child the strategies described in the Strategy section, and then show your child how to solve the various examples presented there by using these strategies.

STEP 3. CHILD: Work on the questions at the end of the Strategy section.

STEP 4. PARENT: Check your child's answers to these questions, and determine whether his or her solutions use the strategies and methods shown in this book. If they don't, explain to your child how to solve the questions using the right strategy.

What Parents Should Know About Standardized Tests

WHAT IS A STANDARDIZED TEST?

By definition, a "standardized test" is a test that is given in the same form to all test takers, and is supposed to measure the same ability for everybody to whom it is given. For example, the test may measure verbal ability or math ability. This means that no matter which child takes the test, that child will obtain a score that measures his or her *verbal* or *math* ability.

The scores in these tests are usually represented in two ways: (1) a scaled score, which is derived from the number of correct answers, and (2) a percentile rank, which lets you know how your child compares with the rest of the test takers. For example, if he or she gets a 60-percentile rank, this means that 39 percent of the test takers scored above your child and 59 percent scored below your child. A 50-percentile rank would mean that your child is right in the middle: that is, just as many scored above your child as scored below.

WHAT IS AN APTITUDE TEST?

Some tests measure *aptitude,* and others measure *achievement.* An *aptitude* test usually has questions that do not require the student to know specific memorizable information such as facts of history, English grammar, science, math, and so on. It usually tests math ability through math skills and logical reasoning, and verbal ability through reading comprehension, analogies, and sentence completions, and vocabulary.

WHAT IS AN ACHIEVEMENT TEST?

An *achievement* test usually has questions that deal with factual information learned in school. However, there is really not a fine line between an achievement and an aptitude test.

HOW ARE APTITUDE TESTS AND ACHIEVEMENT TESTS SIMILAR?

As you will see, one can increase his or her "aptitude" by learning specific critical-thinking skills or strategies, and so do far better on "aptitude" tests. Thus the aptitude test somehow becomes an "achievement" test, since the material tested can be learned. In fact, in recent years some of the test names have actually been changed to reflect this situation. For example, the Aptitude Test of the Graduate Record Examination (a nationwide graduate entrance exam) has recently been changed to Graduate Record Examination, General Test. Even the Scholastic Aptitude Test (given for the last forty years) may be changed to Scholastic Assessment Test for College Entrance.

In this book we will zero in on the most important and common types of questions on standardized tests. They are:

1. Analogies.

This type of test shows whether your child can reason with words. It tests to see whether your child can make meaningful analogies between sets of words. This is perhaps the best way to test *verbal* aptitude or intelligence. Sometimes the questions also test vocabulary, especially if the words in the analogy or in the choices are difficult.

2. Vocabulary.

This type of test shows whether the student knows the meanings of certain words important to his or her projected level of reading and comprehension. The questions that appear can be in many different forms. *Opposites* of words may be tested; *prefixes, suffixes,* or *roots* of words may be tested. A word might also have to be defined based on the *context* of a sentence.

3. Sentence completion.

This type of test determines whether the child can fill in a missing word based on the context of the rest of the sentence. It actually tests two things: reading comprehension and analytical ability. Vocabulary also is sometimes tested.

4. Reading comprehension.

This type of test reveals to what extent your child can comprehend a reading passage. The question may ask the child to recall specific things in the passage; it may ask the child to infer certain things from reading the passage; or it may ask the child to select the best title for the passage. The reading comprehension question can take on many different forms. Usually a passage from fifty to three hundred words is presented with questions that follow. However, your child may be given only a single sentence and a question about the sentence.

5. Writing ability.

This type of test tells you how well your child can write conforming to standard rules of written English. The questions test whether and to what extent your child knows when and how to *capitalize* and *punctuate,* and how to *express a sentence clearly.* The more your child reads, and the more you talk with your child, the more familiar he or she will be with the rules of English and thus be able to express sentences with good English grammar.

MATH

1. Regular math questions.

This is the most common type of math question asked. It is used to test a variety of things. The question may test how well your child is able to compute or calculate something, or whether your child can manipulate certain math quantities effectively, or how well your child can set up or effectively initiate the solution to a math question. Or it may test how well your child reasons using math rules, and how well your child can translate word problems into math format. These questions can also measure whether your child is able to solve a problem the quickest way.

2. Quantitative-comparison.

In these questions, your child is given two quantities, one in Column A and the other in Column B, and he or she has to make a comparison between the columns. This type of question tests how clever your child is in making the comparison, and whether your child can make a comparison with the least amount of calculation or effort. Logical reasoning is measured, since your child has to determine the most logical way of attacking the problem. In these questions, it is very rare that the child will have to tediously calculate quantities. Usually the child can (or should) manipulate the quantities from one column to another to make a comparison. The child who painstakingly *calculates* everything scores lowest on this type of question.

In all math questions, both regular math and the quantitative-comparison, there are two things that your child must do to markedly increase his or her score, and "aptitude." First, your child must learn the most important math concepts and rules (found in this book); second, learn the critical-thinking skills or strategies that will use these concepts and rules. One cannot be done without the other.

Four General Test-Taking Skills

The following skills will help your child make the most efficient use of his or her time during the actual test situation, when seconds or minutes saved can greatly improve his or her score.

1. CODE THE QUESTIONS

When your child is not sure of an answer to a question, he or she should put a question mark before the question number and not spend much time on the question. Your child can always go back to the question if there is time, and he or she will know which questions to go back to by seeing the coded question marks.

Here's an example: (A check [✓] can also be used for questions your child thinks he or she got right.)

EXAMPLE

Choose the word that is closest in meaning to the *capitalized* word:

✓ 1. ADMIRE   (A) work   (B) like   (C) set   (D) hurt
? 2. VAPOROUS   (A) tired   (B) simple   (C) like a gas   (D) hot
✓ 3. VAST   (A) big   (B) simple   (C) broken   (D) close

You should encourage your child to make as many marks on the question paper as he or she needs to. Many students try to keep their question paper clean. That's a mistake. The question papers aren't graded—only the answer sheets.

2. DON'T GET LURED INTO THE CHOICE A CHOICE!

One of the pitfalls confronting all test takers is the tendency to get lured into wrong but good-looking choices, that is, choices that sound correct. And usually this lure is Choice A, because the test makers realize that that's the first choice your child will see. Here's an example:

EXAMPLE

What is the smallest amount of an American coin that is greater in value than a nickel (5¢)?

(A) 6¢   (B) 7¢   (C) 8¢   (D) 9¢   (E) 10¢

Your child may choose 6¢, since 6¢ is greater than 5¢. That's a lure. If your child reads the question more carefully, he or she will realize that what is being described is a <u>coin</u> greater in value than 5¢. That's a dime (10¢). Your child should be wary and think twice about these seemingly easy Choice A answers.

3. DON'T LEAVE ANSWERS BLANK ON THE ANSWER SHEET

Have your child make sure that he or she never leaves an answer blank on the answer sheet. He or she should solidly mark in the answer to each question:

EXAMPLE

1 (A) (B) (C) (D) (E)
2 (A) (B) (C) (D) (E)
3 (A) (B) (C) (D) (E)

For any answer that your child has guessed at, he or she can always put a question mark beside it, so that later he or she can change this answer. The reason for marking every answer is to avoid the possibility of mismarking the answer sheet, by putting the right answer in the wrong box, because of a skipped answer. Your child should answer every question even if there's a penalty for guessing incorrectly, because the penalty is much offset by the probability of a right answer. Your child should never, never leave an answer blank if he or she can eliminate one or more incorrect choices when there's a penalty for guessing.

4. DEVELOP GOOD TIMING

WHEN CERTAIN ABOUT AN ANSWER

If your child feels immediately that one of the choices is correct, he or she shouldn't spend any time looking at the other choices, but should mark the answer sheet with that choice. However, he or she should be sure that the choice is not merely a lure choice (Choice A). If there is no reason to suspect this, your child need not waste time considering other choices that are necessarily incorrect.

WHEN SKIPPING QUESTIONS

Make sure your child knows that if he or she skips a question, he or she must also skip the number on the answer sheet. Your child should make sure that each answer is marked in the space numbered the same as the question being answered.

TOWARD THE END OF THE TEST

When the exam proctor announces that there are, let's say, ten minutes left, your child should complete all the questions he or she can in that time. If there is some time remaining after all the answer boxes have been filled, your child should recheck the answers about which he or she was not sure. It is permitted to change answers on the answer sheet. However, if your child wants to change an answer, he or she should erase the first answer completely, and then fill in the new choice. Your child should always spot-check to see that all answer boxes have only one answer filled in; otherwise the box will be marked wrong, even if one of the answers was correct. Your child should also spot-check the answers to those questions about which he or she was certain, to be sure that the answer was put in the right answer box. He or she should do this with a few answers; this will ensure against losing a whole string of points because of one mismarked answer.

VERBAL STRATEGIES

Before beginning to work on the verbal strategies presented in this part of the book, review the four-step learning method described in the "Introduction to Parents," on page 1.

ANALOGIES

Analogies are used on many standardized tests, and many educators feel that analogies are the best indicators of "intelligence" and "aptitude." Analogies require students to think abstractly and analytically as opposed to working out problems in a rote fashion.

Here is an example of an analogy:

EXAMPLE 1

MAN : BOY : :

    (A) dog : cat
    (B) woman : girl
    (C) person : people
    (D) animal : human

The question really asks the following: MAN is related to BOY in which way? The same way that (A) dog is related to cat, (B) woman is related to girl, etc.

Analogy Strategy: Always Put Analogies in Sentence Form

It is advisable to show your child the best way of attacking analogy questions *before* he or she learns the wrong method. It is very easy to be lured into a wrong but good-sounding answer to an analogy question. For instance, in the example just given, one might at first glance think that MAN is comparable to animal, and BOY to human, and so select Choice D, which is incorrect.

But there's a fail-safe way to answer analogies without ever being lured into the good-sounding but wrong choice: *You put the analogy in the form of a sentence and then find the choice with the words that fit the same sentence form.*

In solving Example 1, you would say, A MAN is a grown-up BOY. Now try each of the choices using the same sentence form:

    (A) A dog is a grown-up cat. This doesn't make sense. So go on to B.
    (B) A woman is a grown-up girl. This sounds good. But go on to C to make sure.
    (C) A person is a grown-up people. Ridiculous. Go to D.
    (D) An animal is a grown-up human. This too is ridiculous.

So the only answer that fits is Choice B, which is the correct answer.

This sentence method is very powerful, and if your child uses it, he or she will never have trouble with analogies. The method will last him or her an academic lifetime, from grade school through graduate school.

Here's a more difficult example:

EXAMPLE 2

PENCIL : PAPER : :

    (A) pen : ink
    (B) crayon : art
    (C) chalk : blackboard
    (D) write : print

Note that if you do not use the sentence method just shown, you can easily be lured into any of the choices, since they all sound like they're associated with the analogy PENCIL : PAPER. Therefore, the most exact sentence possible must be used, and then all the choices tried with the same sentence.

Here's a good sentence: A <u>PENCIL</u> can be used to write on <u>PAPER</u> as . . . Now try the choices.

    (A) A <u>pen</u> can be used to write on <u>ink</u>. This is nonsense.
    (B) A <u>crayon</u> can be used to write on <u>art</u>. This too is ridiculous.
    (C) <u>Chalk</u> can be used to write on a <u>blackboard</u>. This sounds good.
    (D) A <u>write</u> can be used to write on <u>print</u>. This makes no sense either.

Only Choice C works.

Now let's look at a question that was culled from an SAT exam, which is a college entrance exam. You may think that this is too difficult for your child. But as you will see, the ability of your child to prepare early in the game, even with fairly simple analogies, will enable him or her to answer the most difficult analogies! In fact, by the time he or she has to take the SAT, your child might not even have to prepare for it and still do remarkably well!

Here's the question:

EXAMPLE 3

MOTH : CLOTHING : :

    (A) wear : sweater
    (B) hole : closet
    (C) rot : trees
    (D) termite : house

Use the sentence, <u>MOTH</u> attacks <u>CLOTHING</u>. Now try the choices using that sentence.

    (A) <u>Wear</u> attacks a <u>sweater</u>. No.
    (B) <u>Hole</u> attacks a <u>closet</u>. No.
    (C) <u>Rot</u> attacks <u>trees</u>. Yes.
    (D) <u>Termite</u> attacks a <u>house</u>. Yes.

So, which is the correct choice, C or D?

Now you can see why this analogy was on an SAT. But all you really have to do, when two choices look good, is to go back and modify your sentence. Just make your sentence more specific. You would say, A <u>MOTH</u> is an *animal* that attacks <u>CLOTHING</u>.

Now try the choices C and D using that new sentence.

    (C) A <u>Rot</u> is an animal that attacks <u>trees</u>. No!
    (D) A <u>Termite</u> is an animal that attacks a <u>house</u>. Yes!

Choice D is correct.

There is something very interesting about the sentence method. Even if you didn't know the meaning of <u>termite</u> or <u>house</u>, you could still have got the right answer by eliminating the first three choices.

If your child can understand the above analogy, he or she can understand practically any analogy, whether it's on a third or sixth grade test, or a graduate school test!

Most Common Types of Analogies

Here is a list of the most common types of analogies found on standardized tests. It is not important for your child to memorize this list, but it would be a good idea for your child to be aware of these types. Thus when he or she attempts to answer an analogy question, somewhere in your child's mind he or she should realize the type of analogy that will lead to the correct relationship in the analogy.

<u>TYPE OF ANALOGY</u>	<u>TEST EXAMPLE</u>

PART-WHOLE*	LEG : BODY
	    (LEG is *part* of the *whole* BODY.)
	COW : ANIMAL
	    (COW is *part* of the *whole* family of ANIMALS.)

PURPOSE *(what it does)*	SCISSORS : CUT (A SCISSORS is used for the *purpose* of CUTTING.) COPY MACHINE : DUPLICATE (The *purpose* of a COPY MACHINE is to DUPLICATE.)
DEGREE *(how much)*	GRIN : LAUGH (The act of GRINNING is not as *intense* [degree] as LAUGHING.) SHOCKED : SURPRISED (Being SHOCKED is much more *intense* [degree] than being SURPRISED.)
CAUSE-EFFECT *(what happens)*	PRACTICE : IMPROVEMENT (PRACTICE *causes* the *effect* of IMPROVEMENT.) SCOLD : HURT (SCOLDING *causes* the *effect* of HURT in a person.)
OPPOSITE	LIGHT : DARK (LIGHT is the *opposite* of DARK.) ADMIRE : DISLIKE (ADMIRE is the *opposite* of DISLIKE.)
ASSOCIATION *(what you think of when you see this)*	COW : MILK (COWS are *associated* with giving MILK.) BANK : MONEY (A BANK is *associated* with MONEY.)
ACTION-OBJECT *(doing something with or to something else)*	FLY : AIRPLANE (You FLY *[action]* an AIRPLANE.) SHOOT : GUN (You SHOOT *[action]* a GUN.)

CHARACTERISTIC
(what the thing is like)

SANDPAPER : ROUGH
(A main *characteristic* of SANDPAPER is that it's ROUGH.)

CLOWN : FUNNY
(A main *characteristic* of a CLOWN is that he's FUNNY.)

LOCATION OR
HABITAT-OBJECT
(where things are kept or live)

MONKEY : JUNGLE
(A MONKEY *lives* in the JUNGLE.)

CAR : GARAGE
(A CAR is *kept in* a GARAGE.)

USER-TOOL
(what a person uses to create something)

PAINTER : BRUSH
(A PAINTER *uses* a BRUSH.)

PHOTOGRAPHER : CAMERA
(A PHOTOGRAPHER *uses* a CAMERA.)

* All these can work in reverse: That is, you could also have BODY : LEG, ANIMAL : COW, etc., as examples of the type of analogy Whole-Part.

Remember, these examples just given are only for the purpose of making your child familiar with the different and most common types of analogies. Normally when your child attacks an analogy question, he or she will *not verbalize* that the type of analogy is, for example, *purpose.* However, after being exposed to these types, your child will have a better sense of the analogy he or she is dealing with.

Practice Exercises and Explanatory Answers

Have your child try the following analogies (five at a time). Then check his or her answers, which follow the sets of five questions. Go over the answers with your child, making sure that he or she puts the analogy in *sentence form,* as in the examples just shown.

QUESTIONS

1 SCISSORS : CUT : :
- (A) spoon : fork
- (B) hammer : nail
- (C) broom : sweep
- (D) knife : sharpen

2 SAFE : DANGEROUS : :
- (A) wild : frightened
- (B) strong : weak
- (C) long : thin
- (D) angry : sad

3 WATCH : TELEVISION : :
- (A) see : concert
- (B) swim : mile
- (C) hear : head
- (B) listen : radio

4 CAPTURE : LOSE : :
- (A) buy : steal
- (B) push : shove
- (C) develop : destroy
- (D) come : remain

5 BASEBALL : BAT : :
- (A) chess : chessboard
- (B) racetrack : horses
- (C) football : yardline
- (D) tennis : racket

ANSWERS

1 (C) SCISSORS is used to CUT as <u>broom</u> is used to <u>sweep</u>.

2 (B) SAFE is the opposite of DANGEROUS as <u>strong</u> is the opposite of <u>weak</u>.

3 (D) You WATCH TELEVISION as you <u>listen</u> to a <u>radio</u>.
Note: In Choice A, see : concert, you don't really go to a concert to see it, you go to hear it. Thus Choice D is a better choice.

4 (C) CAPTURE is the opposite of LOSE as <u>develop</u> is the opposite of <u>destroy</u>.

5 (D) BASEBALL is played with a BAT as <u>tennis</u> is played with a <u>racket</u>.
In Choice A, chess : chessboard, chess is played with chess pieces, not with a chessboard. In Choice B, racetrack : horses, racetrack is not played with horses.

QUESTIONS

6 RAIN : DRIZZLE : :
- (A) weather : forecast
- (B) gale : breeze
- (C) storm : hurricane
- (D) cloud : sky

7 PICTURE : SEE : :
- (A) television : dial
- (B) play : act
- (C) music : hear
- (D) flower : touch

8 SALMON : FISH : :
    (A) cow : meat
    (B) spider : web
    (C) sparrow : bird
    (D) monkey : cage

9 SCALE : WEIGHT : :
    (A) speedometer : car
    (B) clock : time
    (C) oven : temperature
    (D) telephone : distance

10 GIRAFFE : ZOO : :
    (A) buffalo : Indian
    (B) tropical fish : aquarium
    (C) elephant: jungle
    (D) dinosaur : museum

ANSWERS

6 (B) RAIN is much stronger (degree) than a DRIZZLE. Gale (a heavy wind) is much stronger than a breeze.

7 (C) A PICTURE is for SEEING. Music is for hearing.

8 (C) SALMON is a type of FISH (part of the whole class of fish). A sparrow is a type of bird.

9 (B) The purpose of a SCALE is to measure WEIGHT. The purpose of a clock is to measure time.

10 (B) This is a tricky analogy. A GIRAFFE can be found in the ZOO. Tropical fish can be found in an aquarium.

But what about Choice C and Choice D:

An elephant can be found in a jungle and a dinosaur can be found in a museum!

So you have to modify your sentence to eliminate the incorrect choices:

A GIRAFFE (a *live* animal) can be found in the ZOO, which is *not* the giraffe's *natural habitat.*

Now look at Choice B:

A tropical fish (which is *live*) can be found in an aquarium, which is *not* the fish's *natural habitat.*

Look at Choice C:

An elephant (a *live* animal) can be found in the *jungle,* which is not the elephant's natural habitat. That's false—the jungle *is* the elephant's natural habitat. So Choice C is ruled out.

Look at Choice D:

A <u>dinosaur</u> (which is *not live*—the dinosaurs haven't existed for years!) . . . so that's false. Choice D is ruled out! Thus only Choice B remains.

QUESTIONS

11 HAT : HEAD : :
- (A) glove : hand
- (B) tie : shirt
- (C) dress : lady
- (D) cigarette : mouth

12 TENT : CAMPING : :
- (A) house : running
- (B) job : working
- (C) car : picknicking
- (D) rod and reel : fishing

13 ORANGE : FRUIT : :
- (A) puddle : water
- (B) apple : vegetable
- (C) fly : insect
- (D) meat : dinner

14 POOL : SWIMMING : :
- (A) gymnasium : basketball
- (B) lake : flying
- (C) home plate : baseball
- (D) sword : fencing

15 DOCTOR : PATIENT : :
- (A) lawyer : court
- (B) plumber : toilet
- (C) comedian : joke
- (D) veterinarian : animal

ANSWERS

11 (A) A HAT is worn on the HEAD. A <u>glove</u> is worn on the <u>hand.</u>

12 (D) When you see a TENT, you usually think of CAMPING. When you see a <u>rod and reel</u>, you usually think of <u>fishing</u>. This is an analogy of *association*.

13 (C) ORANGE is a type of FRUIT. <u>Fly</u> is a type of <u>insect.</u>

14 (A) A POOL is where you go SWIMMING. A <u>gymnasium</u> is where you play <u>basketball.</u>

15 (D) A DOCTOR treats and tries to cure PATIENTS. A <u>veterinarian</u> treats and tries to cure <u>animals.</u>
You may have thought that B is also a good choice. But in Choice B, plumber : toilet, toilet is not a living thing, while <u>PATIENT</u> and <u>animal</u> are living things. So Choice D is the best choice.

QUESTIONS

16 CARPENTER : WOOD : :
- (A) electrician : light
- (B) plumber : water
- (C) sculptor : clay
- (D) artist : picture

17 BOW : VIOLIN : :
- (A) compose : piano
- (B) sing : guitar
- (C) strum : banjo
- (D) vibrate : cello

18 LAUGH : SMILE : :
   (A) shout: whistle
   (B) pull: stretch
   (C) hit: tap
   (D) touch : snap

19 GENERAL : ARMY : :
   (A) pilot: airport
   (B) passenger : car
   (C) captain : ship
   (D) singer : orchestra

20 EAT : RESTAURANT : :
   (A) drink : water
   (C) walk : road
   (D) cook : kitchen
   (E) chair : table

ANSWERS

16 (C) A CARPENTER works with WOOD. A <u>sculptor</u> works with <u>clay</u>.
   You may have thought Choice D is good, saying that an <u>artist</u> works with a <u>picture</u>. However, an artist paints a *finished* picture; he or she works with *paints, not pictures.*

17 (C) You BOW a VIOLIN as you <u>strum</u> on a <u>banjo</u>.

18 (C) To LAUGH is a much stronger thing to do than to SMILE. To <u>hit</u> is a much stronger thing to do than to <u>tap</u>.

19 (C) A GENERAL is the leader (commander) of an ARMY. A <u>captain</u> is the leader (commander) of a <u>ship</u>.

20 (C) You primarily EAT in a RESTAURANT as you primarily <u>cook</u> in a <u>kitchen</u>. Suppose you used the sentence, You EAT in a RESTAURANT. Then you'd see that both Choices B and C work with the sentence. Choice B: You <u>walk</u> on a <u>road</u>. Choice C: You <u>cook</u> in a <u>kitchen</u>. So you would have to modify your sentence to make it more exact so that you can zero in on the one correct choice. You would then use the sentence: You *primarily* EAT in a RESTAURANT. Try Choice B: You primarily <u>walk</u> on a <u>road</u>. No! You primarily <u>drive</u> on a road. Choice C: You primarily <u>cook</u> in a <u>kitchen</u>. Yes.

QUESTIONS

21 BUILDING : CITY : :
(A) office : desk
(B) tree : country
(C) house : lake
(D) restaurant : movie

22 THIEF : STEAL : :
(A) actor : drug
(B) criminal : perform
(C) customer : buy
(D) policeman : watch

23 RECTANGLE : FOUR : :
(A) half : two
(B) cent : hundred
(C) triangle : three
(D) score : twenty

24 MOON : EVENING : :
(A) cloud : sky
(B) butter : toast
(C) earth : planet
(D) sun : morning

25 CAT : MEOW : :
(A) bee : sting
(B) horse : cat
(C) cow : milk
(D) frog : croak

ANSWERS

21 (B) BUILDINGS are usually found in CITIES as trees are usually found in the country.

22 (C) A THIEF STEALS. A customer buys.

23 (C) A RECTANGLE has FOUR sides. A triangle has three sides.

24 (D) The MOON comes up in the EVENING. The sun comes up in the morning.

You may have thought a cloud comes up in the sky (Choice A). But a cloud doesn't come *up* in the sky—it is *in* the sky.

25 (D) This can be a tricky one—you have to find the best sentence, so that you won't have more than one choice that works.
Here's a first attempt:

A CAT MEOWS.
Choice A: A bee stings.
Choice D: A frog croaks.

Now change your sentence to make it more exact:

A CAT makes a sound of MEOWING.
Choice A: A bee makes a sound of stinging. No!
Choice D: A frog makes a sound of croaking. Yes!

VOCABULARY

VOCABULARY STRATEGY 1:
Learn Prefixes and Roots

Any educator will tell you that the best way to increase vocabulary is to learn the important *prefixes* and *roots* of words. How many words can be learned from prefixes and roots? Well, studies have shown that the following list of 29 prefixes and 25 roots will give the meaning of over 125,000 words. Not bad for learning just 54 items! Also see Appendix A: Hot Prefixes and Root Words.

This is, of course, just one way to increase vocabulary. The other way is to have your child read as much as he or she can—read anything, from children's books and magazines to newspapers—and *look up words* that are unfamiliar. In the meantime, here are the prefixes and roots:

PREFIXES

PREFIX	MEANING	EXAMPLES
1. ab, a, abs	away from	absent—not to be present, away abscond—to run away
2. ad (also ac, af, an, ap, as, at)	to, toward	adapt—to fit into adhere—to stick to accord—agreement with affect—to imitate annex—to add or join appeal—a request assume—to undertake attract—to draw near
3. anti	against	antifreeze—a substance used to prevent freezing antisocial—refers to somebody who's not social

4.	bi	two	bicycle—a two-wheeled cycle bimonthly—twice monthly
5.	circum, cir	around	circumscribe—to draw around circle—a figure that goes all around
6.	com, con, co, col	with, together	combine—to bring together contact—to touch together collect—to bring together co-worker—one who works with a worker
7.	de	away from, down, the opposite of	depart—to go away from decline—to turn down
8.	dis	apart, not	dislike—not to like dishonest—not honest distant—apart
9.	epi	upon	epitaph—a writing upon a tombstone
10.	equ, equi	equal	equalize—to make equal equitable—fair, equal
11.	ex, e, ef	out, from	exit—to go out eject—to throw out
12.	in, il, ig, ir, im	not	inactive—not active illegal—not legal ignoble—not noble improbable—not probable irreversible—not reversible
13.	in, il, ir, im	into	inject—to put into impose—to force into

illustrate—to put <u>into</u> example

irritate—to put <u>into</u> discomfort

14. inter	between, among	international—<u>among</u> nations interpose—to put <u>between</u>
15. mal, male	bad, wrong, ill	malady—<u>ill</u>ness malfunction—to <u>fail</u> to function; bad functioning malevolent—<u>bad</u>
16. mis	wrong, badly	mistreat—to treat <u>badly</u> mistake—to get <u>wrong</u>
17. mono	one, alone	monopoly—<u>one</u> ownership monologue—speech by <u>one</u> person
18. non	not, the reverse of	nonsense—something that does <u>not</u> make sense nonprofit—<u>not</u> making profit
19. ob	against, in front of, in the way of	obstacle—something that stands <u>in the way of</u> obvious—right <u>in front</u>, apparent
20. omni	everywhere, present everywhere	omnipresent—<u>present</u> <u>everywhere</u>
21. pre	before, earlier than	preview—a viewing that goes <u>before</u> another viewing prehistorical—<u>before</u> written history
22. post	after	postpone—to do <u>after</u> postmortem—<u>after</u> death

23. pro	forward, going ahead of, supporting	proceed—to go forward prowar—supporting the war
24. re	again, back	retell—to tell again recall—to call back
25. sub	under, less than	submarine—boat that goes under water subway—an underground train
26. super	over, above, greater	superstar—a star greater than other stars superimpose—to put something over something else
27. trans	across	transcontinental—across the continent transit—act of going across
28. un	not	unhelpful—not helpful uninterested—not interested
29. un, uni	one	unity—oneness unidirectional—having one direction unanimous—sharing one view

ROOTS

ROOT	MEANING	EXAMPLES
1. act, ag	to do, to act	activity—action agent—one who acts as representative
2. cap, capt, cip, cept, ceive	to take, to hold	captive—one who is held receive—to take capable—to be able to take hold of things

			recipient—one who takes hold reception—the process of taking hold
3.	cede, ceed, cess	to go, to give in	precede—to go before access—a means of going to proceed—to go forward
4.	cred, credit	to believe	credible—believable incredible—not believable credit—belief, trust
5.	curr, curs, cours	to run	current—now in progress, running precursory—running (going) before recourse—to run for aid
6.	dic, dict	to say	diction—verbal saying (expression) indict—to say or make an accusation indicate—to point out or say by demonstrating
7.	duc, duct	to lead	induce—to lead to action aqueduct—a pipe or waterway that leads water somewhere
8.	fac, fact, fic, fect, fy	to make, to do	facile—easy to do fiction—something that has been made up efficient—made effectively satisfy—to make fulfilled factory—a place that makes things affect—to make a change in

9. fer, ferr	to carry, bring	defer—to carry away (put away) referral—the bringing of a source for help or information
10. jec, ject	to throw, to put forward	trajectory—the path of an object that has been thrown project—to put forward
11. lat	to carry, bring	collate—to bring together
12. mit, mis	to send	admit—to send in missile—something that gets sent through the air
13. par	equal	parity—equality disparate—not equal, not alike
14. plic	to fold, to bend, to turn	complicate—to fold (mix) together implicate—to fold in, to involve
15. pon, pos, posit, pose	to place	component—a part placed together with other parts transpose—to place across compose—to put into place many parts deposit—to place for safekeeping
16. scrib, script	to write	describe—to write or tell about transcript—a written copy
17. sequ, secu	to follow	sequence—in following order consecutively—one following another
18. spec, spect, spic	to appear, to look	specimen—an example to look at

		inspect—to look over conspicuous—to appear different; standing out
19. sta, stat, sist, stit	to stand	constant—standing with status—social standing stable—steady (standing) desist—to stand away from constituent—standing as part of a whole

20. tact	to touch	contact—to touch
		  together
		tactile—to be able to be
		  touched

21. ten, tent, tain	to hold	tenable—able to be held;
		  holding
		retentive—holding
		maintain—to keep or
		  hold up

22. tend, tens	to stretch	extend—to stretch or draw out tension—stretched
23. tract	to draw	attract—to draw together contract—an agreement drawn up
24. ven, vent	to come	convene—to come together advent—a coming
25. vert, vers	to turn	avert—to turn away revert—to turn back reverse—to turn around

WORD-DEFINITION EXERCISE—PRACTICE
USING PREFIXES AND ROOTS

Now let's see how many words your child can figure out using prefixes
and roots. Have your child define the following words by looking back
at the list of prefixes and roots. The answers follow. (You may think
these words are too difficult for your child, but you'll be surprised at
how your child can learn the meaning of difficult words, using prefixes
and roots.)

1	circumvent	9	sequel
2	malediction	10	precursory
3	process	11	monotone
4	stationary	12	interject
5	untenable	13	introduce
6	convention	14	recede
7	revert	15	concurrence
8	retract		

ANSWERS

See if your child's answers match these answers.

1 CIRCUMVENT :   CIRCUM   VENT
                        ↓   ↓
                      around   to come → to come around, to
                                              go around
Sentence: The boy cleverly <u>circumvented</u> the real problem.

2 MALEDICTION: MALE   DICT   ION
                        ↓   ↓
                       bad   to say → to say bad things
Sentence: You are always saying <u>maledictions</u> about him.

3 PROCESS: PRO   CESS
                        ↓   ↓
                     forward   go → go forward
Sentence: How do you want to <u>process</u> this order?

4 STATIONARY: STAT   ION   ARY
                          ↓
                     to stand → standing still
Sentence: The stars look like they are <u>stationary.</u>

5 UNTENABLE: UN   TEN   ABLE
                          ↓   ↓
                     not   holding → not holding, flighty
Sentence: This is an <u>untenable</u> situation.

6 CONVENTION: CON   VENT   ION
                          ↓   ↓
                     together   coming → a coming together, a
                                              meeting of many people
Sentence: Let's go to the computer <u>convention.</u>

7 REVERT: RE   VERT
                          ↓   ↓
                     back   turning → turning back, going back
Sentence: Don't <u>revert</u> to your old ways of doing things.

8 RETRACT: RE   TRACT
                          ↓   ↓
                     back   draw → to draw back (to take back)
Sentence: I'm going to <u>retract</u> what I just said about you.

9 SEQUEL: SEQU   EL
                          ↓
                     to follow → following thing
Sentence: Did you see the <u>sequel</u> to *Rocky III*?

10 PRECURSORY: PRE   CURS   ORY
                          ↓   ↓
                     before   running → running before, going
                                              before
Sentence: These are <u>precursory</u> signs of the chicken pox.

11 MONOTONE: MONO   TONE
                          ↓
                     one → one tone
Sentence: Don't talk in such a <u>monotone.</u>

12 INTERJECT: INTER   JECT
                         ↓   ↓

                        between   to put forward → to put between

Sentence: You always <u>interject</u> your own ideas when I'm talking.

13 INTRODUCE: IN   TRO   DUC E
                      ↓   ↓

                      into   to lead → to lead to

Sentence: Could you please <u>introduce</u> me to that girl?

14 RECEDE: RE   CEDE
                      ↓   ↓

                      back → to go → to go back

Sentence: The army <u>receded</u> from its front position.

15 CONCURRENCE: CON   CUR   RENCE
                      ↓   ↓

                      with   running → running with, happening at the same time

Sentence: All these events have a remarkable <u>concurrence</u>.

VOCABULARY STRATEGY 2:
Learn Suffixes

Finally, your child should be familiar with the meanings of certain *suffixes*. Here is a list of some of the important ones:

SUFFIX	MEANING	EXAMPLES
1. able, ible, ble	able to	<u>edible</u>—<u>able to</u> be eaten <u>salable</u>—<u>able to</u> be sold
2. acious, cious, al	like, having the quality of	<u>nocturnal</u>—<u>of the</u> night <u>vivacious</u>—<u>having the quality of</u> being lively
3. ance, ancy	the act of, a state of being	<u>performance</u>—<u>the act of</u> performing <u>truancy</u>—<u>the act of</u> being truant

4. ant, ent, er, or	one who	occup<u>ant</u>—<u>one who</u> occupies respond<u>ent</u>—<u>one who</u> responds teach<u>er</u>—<u>one who</u> teaches creat<u>or</u>—<u>one who</u> creates
5. ar, ary	connected with, related to	ocul<u>ar</u>—<u>related</u> to the eye benefici<u>ary</u>—<u>connected with</u> one who receives benefits
6. ence	the quality of, the act of	exist<u>ence</u>—<u>the act of</u> existing
7. ful	full of	fear<u>ful</u>—<u>full of</u> fear
8. ic, ac, il, ile	of, like, pertaining to	cardi<u>ac</u>—<u>pertaining to</u> the heart civ<u>il</u>—<u>pertaining to</u> citizens infant<u>ile</u>—<u>pertaining to</u> infants acid<u>ic</u>—<u>like</u> acid
9. ion	the act or condition of	correct<u>ion</u>—<u>the act of</u> correcting
10. ism	the practice of, support of	patriot<u>ism</u>—<u>support of</u> one's country
11. ist	one who does, makes	art<u>ist</u>—<u>one who creates</u> art
12. ity, ty, y	the state of, character of	un<u>ity</u>—<u>the state of</u> being one shif<u>ty</u>—<u>state of</u> shifting around show<u>y</u>—the <u>state of</u> always showing oneself
13. ive	having the nature of	act<u>ive</u>—<u>having the nature of</u> acting or moving
14. less	lacking, without	heart<u>less</u>—<u>without</u> a heart

15. logy	the study of	biology—the study of life processes
16. ment	the act of, the state of	retirement—the state of being retired
17. ness	the quality of	eagerness—the quality of being eager
18. ory	having the nature of, a place or thing for	laboratory—a place where work is done
19. ous, ose	full of, having	dangerous—full of danger verbose—full of words or wordy
20. ship	the art or skill of, the ability to	leadership—the ability to lead
21. some	full of, like	troublesome—full of trouble
22. tude	the state or quality of, the ability to	aptitude—the ability to do
23. y	full of, somewhat, somewhat like	musty—having a stale odor chilly—somewhat cold willowy—like a willow

Now that your child has already looked at the section on prefixes and roots, and after you have explained the suffixes with examples, let's see how your child does with these questions. Some involve knowing suffixes only, but others involve a knowing a combination of prefixes, roots, and suffixes.

QUESTIONS

1 What is the meaning of tenacious?

2 What is the meaning of irreversible?

3 What is the meaning of precursor?

4 What is the meaning of unidirectional?

5 What is the meaning of parity?

6 What is the meaning of tactile ?

7 What is the best meaning of the underlined suffix? direc<u>tor</u>
(A) one who (B) place where (C) quality of (D) full of

8 What is the best meaning of the underlined suffix? anthropo<u>logy</u>
(A) being (B) the quality of (C) the study of (D) place where

9 Which is the *prefix* of the following word? <u>inject</u>
(A) i (B) in (C) inj (D) inject

10 Which is the *suffix* of the following word? <u>antagonism</u>
(A) nism (B) ism (C) ant (D) onism

ANSWERS

After you have gone over your child's work for the preceding ten questions, describe how to answer the questions using the following explanations.

1 tenacious: <u>ten</u> = to hold   <u>acious</u> = having the quality of
So <u>tenacious</u> = having the quality of holding on to

2 irreversible: <u>ir</u> = not   <u>re</u> = again, back   <u>vers</u> = turning
<u>ible</u> = able to
So <u>irreversible</u> = not being able to turn back

3 precursor: <u>pre</u> = before   <u>curs</u> = to run   <u>or</u> = one who
So <u>precursor</u> = something that runs before or comes before

4 unidirectional: <u>uni</u> = one   <u>ion</u> = the act of   <u>al</u> = having the quality of
So <u>unidirectional</u> = having the quality of acting in one direction

5 parity: <u>par</u> = equal   <u>ity</u> = the character of
So <u>parity</u> = the state or character of being equal

6 tactile: <u>tact</u> = to touch   <u>ile</u> = pertaining to
So <u>tactile</u> = pertaining to something that can be touched

7 The <u>or</u> in director is the suffix that means *one who* (A).
Director means *one who directs.*

8 The <u>logy</u> in anthropology is the suffix that means *the study of* (C).
Anthropology is *the study of man.*

9 The prefix in the word <u>inject</u> is <u>in</u>. Inject means *to put into.*

10 The suffix of the word <u>antagonism</u> is <u>ism</u>. <u>ism</u> means *the practice of.*

Antagonism means *the practice of antagonizing or hostility.*

Essential Word List for Grades 3 • 4• 5

What follows is a list of 294 words. This list was painstakingly derived from the words *most frequently* found on standardized tests, and contains words your child should know. Have your child look up in the dictionary five words per day. This list purposely does not contain the meanings of these words, because *your child should get used to using the dictionary,* and discover the meaning of the words himself or herself. Have your child check the words for which he or she has already found the meanings.

abandon	attempt	complicated	disorder
abnormal	attitude	composed	disqualify
abolish	audience	conflict	distress
abrupt	authority	consent	donate
absolutely	await	contempt	drowsy
absorb	aware	courier	duplicate
absurd	baffle	creep	durable
abundant	bandit	cruel	earnest
accidentally	blend	cunning	edible
adept	blunder	curb	eliminate
adjust	boast	cured	emergency
admire	bountiful	curiosity	emphasis
adventurous	brevity	customary	encourage
affectionate	brilliant	dally	endorse
alarm	burden	deceive	enormous
alertness	career	decent	erroneous
allegiance	cargo	deface	especially
ample	cavity	demolish	eternal
amplify	cheer	deposit	evade
amused	chore	design	evaporate
annul	coax	detect	evidence
approximately	colossal	dine	exactly
assuredly	command	directory	exaggerate
astounding	comment	discouraged	exhibit
attain	commotion	disguise	exile

expansion	indicate	neglect	reality	token
extensive	intention	negligence	reckon	torment
famous	interest	notable	reduce	trail
fantastic	interfere	notify	refuse	tranquil
fatal	intolerable	obstinate	reliability	treaty
ferocity	intrude	obtain	renown	trek
fertile	invasion	obviously	replenish	triumph
festive	investigate	odd	represent	troublesome
finish	involved	oddity	revise	undoubtedly
firmly	isolation	offend	rival	universally
flavor	juvenile	often	rotated	unravel
fling	keenest	operate	roughly	uproar
flux	kinsman	optimistic	royal	urgent
fortify	knack	orderly	sabotage	valiant
fragrance	lasting	ordinarily	sacrifice	vast
frantic	legend	original	salvage	venture
frigidity	leniently	parch	sarcastic	verdict
fulfill	liberty	particular	savage	vigilance
fundamental	loathe	patiently	savagely	vigorous
gladly	located	peculiar	scheme	violent
global	lofty	peril	seal	vision
gloomy	lonesome	permanent	seldom	visionary
grandeur	loyal	persist	sequence	vocation
grateful	major	persuade	serious	vocational
gratify	margin	petition	shame	volume
guarantee	marvelous	petty	silence	vow
handicap	massive	pomp	smolder	wailing
hesitate	mature	positive	snatch	wary
hew	meager	precious	soil	whole
hindrance	mellow	preliminary	solemn	wholesome
humane	melodious	premature	solitary	withered
husky	menace	prior	soothe	withhold
identify	miniature	proclaim	specific	worthy
ignite	minimum	proper	specifically	yearn
ignore	minstrel	prosperity	stationary	
illiterate	mislead	protest	stranger	
imitate	moist	provision	strenuous	
immense	monopoly	puny	submit	
impatient	murmur	quarreling	swindler	
indecision	mysterious	query	timid	

SENTENCE COMPLETIONS

Sentence completion questions basically test your child's ability to use words correctly in sentences, that is, to fit the right word to the meaning of a particular sentence (or context). There are essentially two types of sentence completion questions. In the first type, there is a sentence in which a word is underlined and its meaning has to be understood from the context in the sentence. In the second type, there is a sentence with a missing word (indicated by a blank), and the correct word must be supplied.

SENTENCE COMPLETION STRATEGY 1: Try All of the Choices

Here's an example of the first type of sentence completion question:

EXAMPLE

He is not <u>convinced</u> that you can do the job on time. <u>Convinced</u> means
   (A) interested
   (B) pushed
   (C) persuaded
   (D) rushed

Here you can try all the choices to see which one fits best in the sentence. That is, of course, if you don't know the meaning of the word <u>convinced</u>.

Try (A): He is not <u>interested</u> that you can do the job on time.
   This is possible but not that good.

Try (B): He is not <u>pushed</u> that you can do the job on time.
   This doesn't make sense.

Try (C): He is not <u>persuaded</u> that you can do the job on time.
   This sounds good.

Try (D): He is not <u>rushed</u> that you can do the job on time.
   This doesn't make sense.

So the best fit is Choice C. Note that if you didn't know what the word underline{persuaded} meant, you could have eliminated the other choices by this method.

Here's an example of the second type of sentence completion question:

EXAMPLE

He did very well on the exam _____ the fact that he hardly studied.
(A) despite
(B) plus
(C) and
(D) except

The easiest way to answer this question is to try each of the choices as you did with the previous example, until you've found the word that seems to fit. For this example, you should know that Choice A (despite) is the right word.

SENTENCE COMPLETION STRATEGY 2: Look for Clues and Key Words

There is, however, a much more accurate method of answering these questions: Look for clues that will suggest the missing word. You can do this by studying the *structure* of the sentence. The sentence says in the example above, "He did well on the exam . . ." and ". . . he hardly studied." You should reason that "hardly studying" somewhat contradicts the fact that "he did well." So the *missing word* is a *link* that describes a *contradiction.* The word/words could be

in spite of
regardless of
despite

You can now see why Choice A fits best.

Here's another example of the second type of sentence completion question:

EXAMPLE

She was really _____ in public, but she was hated at home.
(A) smart
(B) silly
(C) likable
(D) despised

You can, of course, try each choice in the sentence and probably find that Choice C fits. However, it's a good idea to get used to the more effective method, which uses a critical-thinking approach. The word but gives us a clue that while one thing is happening in one part of the sentence, the *opposite* thing is happening in the other. "She was hated at home." "She was really _____ in public." The missing word must be opposite to the word hated. Choice C describes a good opposite.

Sentence Completion Exercises and Explanatory Answers

The following are examples of the first type of sentence completion problem. Have your child do these after you have explained to him or her the strategies just described.

QUESTIONS

1 Some items are made to last a lifetime, whereas others are made to be quickly consumed.

The word consumed means
(A) to be used up
(B) to be praised
(C) to be eaten
(D) to be sold

2 In order to find out what caused the disease, the doctors had to isolate the disease germs.

Isolate means
(A) intensify
(B) separate
(C) calculate
(D) destroy

3 Because he cheated on the exam, he was penalized by losing 20 points.

Penalized means
(A) gratified
(B) pardoned
(C) supported
(D) punished

4 Everybody understood exactly what he was saying because he gave such a lucid speech.

Lucid means
(A) vibrant
(B) slow
(C) clear
(D) wild

5 John has to travel many hours to his job because he resides far from where he works.

Resides means
(A) travels
(B) lives
(C) plays
(D) comes

ANSWERS

After your child tries the preceding exercises, explain the answers below to him or her, and check to see how your child approached each question.

1 (A) "Some items are made to last a lifetime, <u>whereas</u> others . . ." <u>Whereas</u> tells us that others will not last a lifetime, Thus the word <u>consumed</u> must mean <u>to be used up.</u>

2 (B) If your child does not know the meaning of the word <u>isolate</u>, it is best to have your child *eliminate* the incorrect choices. Put each of the choices in the sentence:

(A) . . . the doctors had to <u>intensify</u> the disease germs. It is unlikely that the doctors would want to <u>intensify</u> the germs in order to find a cure. Therefore Choice A is wrong.

(B) . . . the doctors had to <u>separate</u> the disease germs. This sounds as if they can then find out about the individual germs—so far a good choice.

(C) . . . the doctors had to <u>calculate</u> the disease germs. You don't calculate disease germs—you calculate the *number* of disease germs. Choice C is incorrect.

(D) . . . the doctors had to <u>destroy</u> the disease germs. You'd want to destroy the germs to make the patient better, but the doctors were trying to find out *what caused the disease.* If they destroyed the germs, they wouldn't be able to figure out what caused them. So Choice D is incorrect.

Choice B is the only remaining good choice.

3 (D) "Because he cheated on the exam," something bad happened to him—he lost 20 points. Thus he must have been <u>punished.</u> He certainly wasn't gratified (Choice A), pardoned (Choice B), or supported (Choice C).

4 (C) If everybody knew what the speaker was talking about, the speaker must have given a very clear, understandable speech. <u>Lucid</u> must mean <u>clear.</u>

5 (B) If John travels many hours to and from his job, he must <u>live</u> very far from where he works. Choice B is therefore correct.

QUESTIONS

Now have your child try the following exercises, which are examples of the second type of sentence completion problem. (Find the missing word.)

1 Although she is really_____, she does not do well on exams.
(A) likable
(B) smart
(C) rich
(D) stupid

2 Don't live in a dreamworld— you can't make money without putting in a lot of_____.
(A) enjoyment
(B) happiness
(C) structure
(D) effort

3 It's one thing to have ideas, but it's another thing to_____ them into something.
(A) destroy
(B) push
(C) plan
(D) develop

4 The weather looks slightly gray outside. It might _____ .
(A) rain
(B) storm
(C) pour
(D) hail

5 That was the best time I've ever had away from home, and to think I didn't even want to ____.
(A) stay
(B) play
(C) go
(D) arrive

ANSWERS

After your child tries the preceding exercises, go over his or her work and explain the following answers.

1 (B) Although is a key word in the sentence. It tells us that something happens even though something else happens. So we are looking for *opposites*. The phrase "she does not do well on exams" makes us believe that she may not be intelligent. But the word although in the sentence contradicts that and is saying that she is smart. Choice B is the correct answer.

2 (D) If you did live in a dream world, you might think that money grows on trees or that you would have to put very little effort into making money. Choice D is therefore correct.

3 (D) The sentence is really saying that it's great to have ideas but you should do something with them. What can you do? You can <u>develop</u> them into something. Choice D is therefore correct.

4 (A) The key word in the sentence is "<u>slightly</u>." If the weather looks only "<u>slightly gray</u>" outside, it then might only <u>rain.</u> It is unlikely that it will <u>storm, pour,</u> or <u>hail</u>. Choice A is the answer.

5 (C) The person is saying that because he or she had a great time— it's a good thing he or she went. So when the person says "and to think I didn't even want to_____," the blank word must be <u>go</u> (Choice C). It couldn't have been <u>stay</u> (Choice A). <u>Play</u> (Choice B) is too specific in the context of the first part of the sentence. <u>Arrive</u> (Choice D) does not make sense.

READING COMPREHENSION
(Two Strategies)

Reading comprehension questions test the general ability to understand what a passage is about. Four specific abilities are also tested:

1. Formulating the main idea:
> the ability (a) to select the main idea in a passage, and (b) to select the best title for the passage.

2. Spotting details:
> the ability (a) to understand specific references or sections in a passage, and (b) to identify specific parts in the passage.

3. Drawing inferences:
> the ability (a) to weave together ideas in a passage in order to see their relationships, and (b) to infer things about the passage even though they may not be directly stated.

4. Identifying tone or mood:
> the ability to figure out the tone or mood of a passage—serious, sad, funny, and so on.

The following are some typical questions asked of reading comprehension passages:

QUESTION	ABILITY (1–4 ABOVE)
1. According to the passage, the reason why the . . .	2 (or 1)
2. The best title for the passage would be . . .	1
3. Which of the following would the author probably describe next?	3
4. The tone throughout the passage is primarily one of . . .	4
5. The main concern of the writer is . . .	1
6. The word warmonger in line 5 refers to . . .	2
7. The passage implies that John was . . .	3
8. The author's attitude toward Sam is best described as . . .	4 (or 2)

There are two main strategies that can be employed in reading comprehension questions.

READING STRATEGY 1: While you read the passage, be aware of the four abilities described above.

READING STRATEGY 2: Underline key parts or sentences or words in the passage, so that you'll be able to spot things quickly in the passage when answering the questions. Underline and make notes about (1) main idea, (2) details, (3) inferences, and (4) tone or mood. Particularly underline parts of a passage which seem important or interesting.

Here's a reading passage followed by several questions. First, read the passage and answer the questions. Then look at the explanatory answers to the questions. After you have got a feel for how to answer the questions strategically, have your child read the passage and answer the questions. Go over the answers with your child, making sure that he or she answers the questions strategically (as explained in the answers given below).

When I was young, I remember how much better things were made. Things were not made of cheap plastic but of metal. You got a feeling you had something solid, rather than something that would last only a few months. I remember when Uncle Harry banged his car into a wall, it hardly had a dent. But now you can just barely hit a car and you see some very visible damage. The trouble is that nobody complains. People are satisfied with poorer materials even though they might even be more expensive than the previous cheaper ones. Or maybe people fool themselves into thinking that the newer items are better. After all, metal rusts, plastic is lighter to carry, and most people have good car insurance.

QUESTIONS AND ANSWERS

Let's see how to answer the following questions:

1 The tone of the last two sentences in the passage is
    (A) contradictory (saying the opposite about something)
    (B) sad
    (C) sarcastic (poking fun at)
    (D) angry

To find the correct answer, we have to realize that throughout most of the passage, the author was very pro to the "old" materials, saying that they were built better, you had something solid, and so on. So at the end of the passage, the author is <u>poking fun at</u>, or being <u>sarcastic</u> about what people might say to justify why things are so poorly made. The last two sentences are not meant to be contradictory, but sarcastic. Choice C is correct.

2 Which statement can be inferred from the passage?
    (A) Things were more expensive a long time ago.
    (B) Fewer people owned cars when the author was young.
    (C) People now don't complain as much as when the author was young.
    (D) Plastic is now substituted for metal in many items.

Before trying to answer this question, read the underlinings in the passage below and review Reading Strategies 1 and 2, which were discussed above.

UNDERLININGS YOU SHOULD DO

When I was <u>young</u>, I remember <u>how much better things were made</u>. Things were <u>not made of cheap plastic but of metal</u>. You got a feeling you had <u>something solid</u>, rather than something that would <u>last</u> only a <u>few months</u>. I remember when Uncle Harry banged his car into a wall, it hardly had a dent. But now you can just barely hit a car and you see some very visible damage. The trouble is that <u>nobody complains</u>. People are <u>satisfied with poorer materials</u> even though they might even be more expensive than the previous cheaper ones. Or <u>maybe people fool themselves</u> into thinking that the newer items are better. After all, metal rusts, plastic is lighter to carry, and most people have good car insurance.

Now let's look at each choice for question 2.

    (A) The author states that, if anything, things are more expensive now than they were when the author was young. So Choice A is incorrect.
    (B) Just because people now have good car insurance doesn't mean that fewer people owned cars when the author was young. Choice B is incorrect.
    (C) Just because nobody complains now doesn't mean that they didn't complain about things when the author was young.
    (D) See line 2. "Things were not made of cheap plastic but of metal." It is then implied that cheap plastic is substituted now for metal. Choice D is correct.

3 In the last line when the author says that "most people have good car insurance," the author is trying to be
   (A) understanding
   (B) humorous
   (C) pointless
   (D) fearless

The author says that most people have good car insurance in a sarcastic and *humorous* way. This is funny because of something that the author said before: that his Uncle Harry banged his car into a wall but didn't really dent it. The author then says that now cars are easily dented. So if most people now have good car insurance, they shouldn't be worried if the car is made poorly.

4 According to the passage, which would the author most likely want to see happen?
   (A) That people would complain about the quality of things and that something would be done about it.
   (B) That people would not fool themselves anymore about the quality of things.
   (C) That cars would be built all of metal.
   (D) That things would be cheap, as they might have been when the author was young.

There are two main ideas in the passage. One is the author's feeling that things were much better built when the author was young; the second is that people don't complain, or they fool themselves, so that things don't get back to where they were. So the author would most likely agree with Choice A. Although the author might like to see happen what is described in Choice B, he would *most likely want to see* what's happening in Choice A. Thus Choice B is incorrect. Choice C is incorrect, and Choice D is not a concern of the author.

In summary:

1 Make sure that your child gets the gist of the passage—what is consistently being described. This will give him or her insight into the main idea or title of the passage.

2 Underline those parts of the passage that you feel may be important or required for referral later. The question will not usually repeat or refer to exactly what is in the passage, but it will mention some part of what you read.

3 Often a specific thing will be mentioned, and from this you must *infer* something more general. For example, with reference to question 2 above, the passage says that when the author was young, things were not made of cheap plastic but of metal. If that is so, we have to *infer* that today plastic is often substituted for metal.

Reading Passages, Questions, and Explanatory Answers

Have your child read the passages below and answer the reading comprehension questions that follow each passage. Then check to see whether his or her answers match those that are given in the book. Also check to see whether your child underlined the passage in the same way as was done in the book. It is not necessary to have the exact same underlinings as long as your child answered the questions accurately. If your child can comprehend the passage *without* underlining and did well with the questions, don't worry about the underlining. You may want to tell your child that it is advisable to underline, in case he or she needs to refer to specific details that he or she normally would not remember.

> The school principal was offering a gold pen to anyone who could drop an egg from the roof of the school without the egg breaking.
> Sally made a parachute from an old cloth and tied the cloth to a plastic cup. To protect the egg from hard knocks, she lined the cup with cotton balls, putting the egg inside the cup.
> Everybody made some sort of contraption, but Sally's was by far the most interesting and promising. Everybody dropped their egg-contraption. When Sally dropped hers, there was a strong breeze at the time, but the parachute opened smoothly. A little ways down, however, the plastic cup turned upside down and the egg fell out and broke on the ground.
> Although nobody won the prize, Sally had realized how to improve on her contraption, was excited to try again, and was determined that she would win the prize the next try.

QUESTIONS

1 Which is the best title for the story?
(A) "The Broken Egg"
(B) "A Strange Contest"
(C) "Sally's Parachute"
(D) "The Strong Breeze"

2 What could have made the cup turn over?
(A) too small an egg
(B) possible collapse of the parachute
(C) the wind
(D) cotton balls in the wrong place in the cup

3 What was Sally's feeling after her egg broke on the ground?
(A) surprise
(B) anger
(C) sadness
(D) encouragement

4 What prize was being offered to the winner?
(A) an egg
(B) a new cloth
(C) a parachute
(D) a pen

5 The word "promising" in the third paragraph of the story refers to
(A) the principal guaranteeing the winner a golden pen
(B) the feeling that nobody would win the prize
(C) Sally's parachute invention
(D) Sally's determination of winning

6 Which is an assumption and not a fact in the story?
(A) The principal was offering a golden pen to the winner.
(B) Nobody won the prize.
(C) There was a strong breeze when Sally dropped her egg.
(D) Sally would win the contest next try.

ANSWERS

Compare the following answers with those of your child. Make sure that your child understands these explanations, and why the wrong answers are wrong.

1 (C) The story really describes the cleverness of Sally's parachute. This idea is present everywhere in the story and is the main theme of the story.

Wrong Choices:
(A) The broken egg only occurs at the end of the story and is not the focus of interest throughout the story.
(B) Certainly this was a strange contest, but that is not the chief element in the story—it is the parachute contraption that gets our interest.
(D) The strong breeze only occurred in one part of the story and although it might have been the cause of the cup turning, it is not the main attraction or theme of the story.

2 (C) Look at the wording in the story: "When Sally dropped hers, there was a strong breeze at the time, but the parachute opened smoothly. A little ways down, however, the plastic cup turned upside down..." The word however tells us that even though the parachute opened smoothly, the breeze later affected the cup.

Wrong Choices:
(A) Too small an egg would not make the cup turn over.
(B) The parachute opened smoothly but even if the parachute collapsed, due to the wind, it wouldn't make the cup turn over. It would just make the cup go down faster.

(D) Cotton balls are so light that even if they were in the wrong place in the cup, they would not make the cup turn over.

3 (D) After her egg broke, the story says (in the last paragraph), Sally realized how to improve her contraption, and was excited to try again. She was also determined that she would win on the next try. This all indicates <u>encouragement</u>, not (A) surprise, or (B) anger or (C) sadness.

4 (D) The beginning of the story says that the principal was offering a <u>gold pen</u> to the winner.

Wrong Choices:
(A) Although students were dropping eggs, that wasn't the prize.
(B) Although Sally used an old cloth for her parachute, that wasn't the prize.
(C) Although Sally made a parachute, that wasn't the prize.

Parent: Note that Choices A, B, and C try to lure the student who has superficially read the passage and casually just caught the words <u>egg</u>, <u>cloth</u>, <u>parachute</u> in the passage.

5 (C) Look at the third paragraph. It says that "Sally's was by far the most interesting and <u>promising</u>." This refers to Sally's parachute contraption. Although the word <u>promising</u> can generally refer to Choices A, B, and D also, the word <u>promising</u> *in the third paragraph* cannot. Therefore Choices A, B, and D are incorrect.

6 (D) Although Sally was determined that she would win on the next try (last paragraph), this is an *assumption* and *not a fact*. Thus Choice D is correct.

Wrong Choices:
(A) It is a *fact* that the principal was offering a golden pen to the winner (beginning).
(B) It is a *fact* that nobody won the prize (see last paragraph).
(C) It is a *fact* that there was a strong breeze when Sally dropped her egg (see third paragraph).

Parent: You should realize that in many of these questions the student has to be very exact in his or her analysis. The student cannot base answers on his or her own assumptions or feelings, but must base them on what is in the story. For example, in question 3, although your child's feeling might have been one of *anger* when the egg broke, this was not Sally's feeling. And it is *Sally's feeling* that is asked for in the question.

Let's look at another passage:

High in the Swiss Alps long years ago, there lived a lonely shepherd boy who longed for a friend to share his vigils. One night, he beheld three wrinkled old men, each holding a glass. The first said: "Drink this liquid and you shall be victorious in battle."

The second said: "Drink this liquid and you shall have countless riches."

The last man said: "I offer you the happiness of music—the alphorn."

The boy chose the third glass. Next day, he came upon a great horn, ten feet in length. When he put his lips to it, a beautiful melody floated across the valley. He had found a friend. . . .

So goes the legend of the alphorn's origin. Known in the ninth century, the alphorn was used by herdsmen to call cattle, for the deep tones echoed across the mountainsides. And even today, on a quiet summer evening, its music can be heard floating among the peaks.

Now have your child answer the following questions, and compare his or her answers with the explanatory answers below.

QUESTIONS

1 The story tells us that of the three old men, the one whose glass the boy chose was the
(A) smallest in size
(B) most wrinkled
(C) first to speak
(D) oldest
(E) last to speak

2 One liquid offered to the boy would have brought him
(A) defeat in battle
(B) great wealth
(C) lonely vigils
(D) another boy to help him
(E) three wishes

3 To the boy, the alphorn
(A) seemed too heavy to play
(B) seemed like a real friend
(C) brought unhappiness
(D) sounded unpleasant
(E) brought great riches

4 The practical use of the alphorn is to
(A) summon the three old men
(B) make friends
(C) call cattle
(D) give summer concerts
(E) tell the legends of the Alps

UNDERLININGS

High in the Swiss Alps long years ago, there lived a lonely shepherd boy who longed for a friend to share his vigils. One night, he beheld three wrinkled old men, each holding a glass. The first said: "Drink this liquid and you shall be victorious in battle."

The second said, "Drink this liquid and you shall have countless riches."

The last man said: "I offer you the happiness of music—the alphorn."

The boy chose the third glass. Next day, he came upon a great horn, ten feet in length. When he put his lips to it, a beautiful melody floated across the valley. He had found a friend. . . .

So goes the legend of the alphorn's origin. Known in the ninth century, the alphorn was used by herdsmen to call cattle, for the deep tones echoed across the mountainsides. And even today, on a quiet summer evening, its music can be heard floating among the peaks.

ANSWERS

1 (E) Look at the underlinings. The boy chose the third glass from the last man to speak.

2 (B) Look at the underlinings. The first glass offered victory in battle. The second, countless riches; the third, happiness of music. Countless riches is great wealth; thus Choice B is correct.

3 (B) See the underlinings. When the boy heard the music, he knew that he had found a friend, so the alphorn seemed like a real friend to him.

4 (C) See the underlinings. The alphorn was used to call cattle.

WRITING ABILITY

Questions testing writing ability usually are designed to see whether your child can *punctuate, capitalize,* and *express a sentence correctly.*

Instead of you or your child having to wade through a set of tedious grammar, capitalization, and punctuation rules, you are only going to see some sentences that are incorrect, which you will then learn how to correct. You are only going to work with the most important and typical sentences and corrections, so that your child, with the least amount of effort, should be able to answer many questions involving grammatical rules and writing techniques.

Punctuation

Here are some typical sentences needing correct <u>punctuation</u>. Look at them, and then the correct punctuation will be shown. Go over these and the corrections with your child.

QUESTIONS

1 The sports that I like best are baseball soccer and tennis.

2 After much talk we all decided to give the party on Tuesday May 5 2009

3 Harry John and Phil went to Bobs house.

4 Let me out of the car its going too fast Susan said

5 Dear Susan

   Thank you for the gift the flowers which you had sent

   Truly yours

   Bill

6 New York is well known for its large skyscrapers crowded streets and good restaurants

7 Hey Paul Sam yelled who are you going to take to the dance

8 This couldnt have happened to Jim because hes such a kind person

9 Here are the results John 30 points Sam 50 points and Paul 20 points

10 As the car approached the hotel all of Martins family ran out to greet the Potters

11 If you want to do well study if you want to do poorly dont study

ANSWERS

Here are the sentences with the correct punctuation:

1 The sports that I like best are baseball, soccer, and tennis. For three or more words in series, use commas except after "and." Use period to end sentence.

2 After much talk, we all decided to give the party on Tuesday, May 5, 2009. A comma is usually used after a phrase or clause that begins a sentence. Use comma after days and dates.

3 Harry, John, and Phil went to Bob's house.
For three or more words in series, use commas. Use apostrophe to show possession: <u>Bob's house</u> = house of Bob.

4 "Let me out of the car—it's going too fast," Susan said. Use quotes (") for direct quotation. Sandwich comma between last word of quotation and quotation marks. Use dash to indicate final clause that explains or summarizes ideas. Use apostrophe for contraction: <u>it's</u> = it is.

5 Dear Susan,

Thank you for the gift (the flowers) which you had sent.

Truly yours,

Bill

Use comma or colon (:) after "Dear [Name]." Use parenthesis ( ) to show a clarification of what precedes. End with "Truly yours," or "Sincerely yours," etc. Then write your name below.

6 New York is well known for its large skyscrapers, crowded streets, and good restaurants.
For three or more words in series, use commas except after "and."

7 "Hey, Paul!" Sam yelled. "Who are you going to take to the dance?"
For clarity, separate Hey and Paul by using a comma. Use quotation marks (") for direct quotation. Use exclamation point (!) for strong emotion or warning. Sandwich exclamation point between last word of quotation and quotation marks. Use question mark (?) for question-type sentences. Sandwich question mark between last word of quotation and quotation marks.

8 This couldn't have happened to Jim because he's such a kind person.
Use apostrophes in contractions: couldn't = could not; he's = he is.

9 Here are the results: John—30 points, Sam—50 points, and Paul—20 points.
Use dashes to show relation to preceding word and to clarify meaning. Use colon (:) when tabulating something and before what seems like a full sentence.

10 As the car approached the hotel, all of Martin's family ran out to greet the Potters.
A comma is usually used after a phrase or clause that begins a sentence. Use apostrophe to show possession: Martin's family = family of Martin.

11 If you want to do well, study; if you want to do poorly, don't study.
A comma is usually used after a phrase or clause that begins a sentence. Use semicolon (;) to separate independent clauses. Use apostrophe for contraction: don't = do not.

TEN PUNCTUATION QUESTIONS

Have your child answer the following questions. Go over your child's answers and compare them with the answers given after the question section. Then show your child how to correct his or her mistakes. You may want to explain to your child the directions to the questions.

Directions: In each of these sentences there may be an error in punctuation. If there is an error, choose the underlined part that should be changed in order to make the sentence correct. No sentence has more than one error, and some have none. If there is no error choose D.

EXAMPLE

Philip, John, and, Joe went outside to play. No error.
　　　A　　　B　　　C　　　　　　　　　　　D

Here you would choose C since the underlined comma marked C is incorrect. There should be no comma after the word "and."

EXAMPLE

"Don't you understand how to do this?" _asked Mr. Martin.
      A   B C

No error.
   D

Here you would choose D since there is <u>no error</u>.

QUESTIONS

1 A porcupine, looking for shelter, found a snakes cave deep in the
            A   B   C
woods. <u>No error.</u>
            D

2 Already late for school, the boy cried frantically, "Mother, where
                          A   B   C
is my lunch?" <u>No error.</u>
                   D

3 Mr. Jones, who teaches at Public School 248, likes to prepare his
          A   B
family's meals. <u>No error.</u>
        C   D

4 "We're very fond of you", said the coach, "but you aren't fast
      A   B   C
enough to make the team." <u>No error.</u>
                              D

5 Serve a pork roast with gravy, baked potato, sweet peas, and,
                              A   B   C
carrots. <u>No error.</u>
             D

6 It was discovered that about seventy-five million households in

the United States, or, 98 percent, own at least one television set.
            A   B   C

<u>No error.</u>
   D

7 "There is no time to argue," he said, "This is the time for action."
      A   B   C

<u>No error.</u>
   D

8 We're good at certain sports, such as: tennis, swimming, and
    A   B   C

  track. No error.
        D

9 My sister, whos younger than I am, can work longer and harder
          A   B   C

  than I can. No error.
          D

10 "Help! he cried as Silver Lake's current pulled him downward.
    A   B   C

   No error.
       D

ANSWERS

1 (C) snake's

2 (D) no error

3 (D) no error

4 (C) you," (put comma *inside* quotation mark)

5 (C) and carrots (no comma after "and")

6 (B) or 98 percent (no comma after "or")

7 (C) said. (period after "said")

8 (B) as tennis (no colon after "as")

9 (B) who's (who's = who is)

10 (A) "Help!" (quotation marks before *and after* ("Help!")

Capitalization

Below are some typical sentences needing correct *capitalization*. Look at them, and then the correct capitalization will be given. Go over these sentences and the corrections with your child.

QUESTIONS

1 The play is about a man who plays the cello for the san francisco symphony in california.

2 "if you are going to the market," Said uncle henry, "Why not get me some Pipe Tobacco?"

3 The Film *great trains of the forties* will be shown in december at beacon hill.

4 "because studying demands concentration" Said the Teacher, "i want you to do your homework in a quiet room."

5 "oh Yes!" Said bill. "you always use a pencil on these Tests."

6 The Waiter spoke only german, but the Chef could speak five Languages.

7 The place in our Nation where presidents are carved in stone is mount rushmore.

8 The restaurant prided itself on its chef who made cakes in the shape of the George Washington bridge.

9 *A tale of two cities* is a book about the French revolution.

10 For its project, professor Hart's class wrote a booklet entitled "the great thinkers of the century."

11 "Sincerely Yours" and "Yours Truly" are two of the ways to close a Personal Letter.

ANSWERS

Here are the sentences with the correct capitalization.

1 The play is about a man who plays the cello for the <u>S</u>an <u>F</u>rancisco <u>S</u>ymphony in <u>C</u>alifornia.
   <u>C</u>apitalize names of organizations and cities, states, or countries.

2 "<u>I</u>f you are going to the market," <u>s</u>aid <u>U</u>ncle <u>H</u>enry, "<u>w</u>hy not get me some <u>p</u>ipe <u>t</u>obacco?"
   <u>C</u>apitalize all words at the beginning of a sentence. Capitalize titles like Uncle, President, when used with a name.

3 The film *<u>G</u>reat <u>T</u>rains of the <u>F</u>orties* will be shown in <u>D</u>ecember at <u>B</u>eacon <u>H</u>ill.
   <u>C</u>apitalize words, except transition words like *in* and *the,* in any title. Capitalize all names of places such as streets: Beacon Hill. Capitalize the names of the months.

4 "Because studying demands concentration," said the teacher, "I want you to do your homework in a quiet room."
Capitalize all first words: said is not capitalized because it is not the beginning of a sentence. I is always capitalized, teacher is not capitalized because it is not a name of someone and refers generally to that profession.

5 "Oh yes!" said Bill. "You always use a pencil on these tests."
You do not capitalize yes because it is not the first word in the sentence. Bill is a personal name and is capitalized. You don't capitalize tests because tests is not a proper name.*

6 The waiter spoke only German, but the chef could speak five languages.
You capitalize the names of languages like German but don't capitalize the word language. The words waiter and chef are not names of people and they are not capitalized.

7 The place in our nation where presidents are carved in stone is Mount Rushmore.
The word nation is not capitalized—it is not the proper* name of something. The word presidents is not capitalized because it is not next to an actual president's name. Mount Rushmore is capitalized because it is the name of a place.

8 The restaurant prided itself on its chef who made cakes in the shape of the George Washington Bridge.
The whole title of the bridge is capitalized—George Washington Bridge.

9 *A Tale of Two Cities* is a book about the French Revolution.
Titles are capitalized, except for transitional words like *of, the, in,* and so on. The complete name French Revolution is capitalized.

10 For its project, Professor Hart's class wrote a booklet entitled "The Great Thinkers of the Century."
You always capitalize a personal title when next to a name—Professor Hart's. Titles of books, magazines, booklets, and so on are always capitalized, except for transition words. Thus you have "The Great Thinkers of the Century."

11 "Sincerely yours" and "Yours truly" are two of the ways to close a personal letter.
You don't capitalize the second word in a closing. Personal letter does not refer to a title so it is not capitalized.

*A proper noun (or name) names a particular person, place or thing—the Statue of Liberty, Cesar Chavez, etc.

TEN CAPITALIZATION QUESTIONS

Have your child answer the following questions. Go over your child's answers and compare them with the answers given following the question section. Then show your child how to correct his or her mistakes. You may want to explain to your child the directions to the questions.

Directions: In each of these sentences there may be an error in capitalization. If there is an error, choose the underlined part that should be changed in order to make the sentence correct. No sentence has more than one error and some have none. If there is no error, choose D.

EXAMPLE

Philip, John, and Joe went outside to Play. No error.
    A   B   C   D

Here you would choose C, since the underlined letter marked C is incorrect. The word play should not be capitalized.

EXAMPLE

"Don't you understand how to do this?" asked Mr. Martin. No error.
   A   B C   D

Here you would choose D since there is no error.

QUESTIONS

1 Was Ronald Reagan the oldest person ever to be elected president
                              A   B

of this country? No error.
    C   D

2 Harry and I were fascinated with the song "Blowing in the
         A   B

wind." No error.
 C   D

3 Dear Mr. Samuels:
   Thank you for letting me know about your cancellation on
                                      A

Monday.

                               Yours Truly,
                               B   C

                               Dr. Charles Widmer No error.
                                             D

4 The Society <u>of</u> Carpenters is now holding <u>meetings</u> to show <u>people</u>
             A   B   C
how to work with wood. <u>No error.</u>
                               D

5 The <u>climates</u> of the <u>Countries</u> Argentina, Norway, and <u>Spain</u> are
        A   B   C
quite different. <u>No error.</u>
                       D

6 Camping in <u>Massachusetts</u> can be delightful, especially in the <u>Fall</u>
               A   B
of the <u>year.</u> <u>No error.</u>
       C   D

7 The rains were heavy in Texas because some heavy winds

originated from the <u>gulf</u> <u>of</u> <u>Mexico.</u> <u>No error.</u>
                     A   B C   D

8 The Marin County Chamber of <u>Commerce</u> has information for
                                A
anyone interested in knowing about <u>annual</u> <u>wine</u> festivals starting
                                       B   C
Monday, April 15. <u>No error.</u>
                      D

9 Our <u>Doctor</u> has an office on Market <u>Street</u> near Fidelity Savings
        A   B
and <u>Loan.</u> <u>No error.</u>
      C   D

10 The <u>author's</u> <u>assistant</u> spoke German and English, but also could
         A   B
understand some of the other <u>Languages.</u> <u>No error.</u>
                              C   D

ANSWERS

1 (D) No error (<u>person</u>, <u>president</u>, and <u>country</u> are not names).

2 (C) <u>Wind</u> is capitalized because it is part of the title of the song but is not a transitional word.

3 (C) The word <u>truly</u> is not capitalized—only the first word of the closing is.

4 (D) No error.

5 (B) Because it is not a proper name, <u>countries</u> is not capitalized.

6 (B) The word <u>fall</u> is not capitalized—it is not the proper name of something.

7 (A) <u>Gulf</u> is capitalized because it is part of the name <u>Gulf of Mexico</u>. Notice that <u>of</u> is not capitalized because it is a transitional word.

8 (D) <u>Commerce</u> is capitalized because it is part of the proper name—<u>The Marin County Chamber of Commerce</u>. <u>Annual</u> and <u>wine</u> are not capitalized because they refer to general festivals, not specific ones.

9 (A) Since it is not next to a name, <u>doctor</u> is not capitalized. <u>Street</u> is capitalized because it is next to a name, <u>Market</u>. <u>Loan</u> is capitalized, since it is part of the title <u>Fidelity Savings and Loan</u>.

10 (C) The word <u>languages</u> is not capitalized; it is not the name of a language.

English Expression

TYPICAL SENTENCES WITH WORDING PROBLEMS

Here are some typical sentences with problems in wording. Look at them, and then go on to read the correct sentences, which follow. Then, show these sentences to your child and explain the corrections to him or her.

QUESTIONS

1 Because I had to go to bed early, I would like to have my friends to leave the party as early as possible.

2 The waves in the ocean is very high certain time of the days.

3 Mrs. Martins was so angry at his brother and he that she took his allowances away that week.

4 That's a real fast car that John and Paul drives.

5 He would buy the toy if he has enough money.

6 Harry and John will take there dog wherever they are likely to goes.

7 Where their is a will, there is a way.

8 John has never been so scared like he was on Thursday night.

9 George and Jim is very careful about not to spill anything.

10 Last Friday, gobs of rain pours down the windows sills.

11 All the kittens in the litter was for sale.

ANSWERS

Here are the sentences with the correct wording:

1 Because I <u>have</u> to go to bed early, I would like to have my friends <u>leave</u> the party as early as possible.
<u>had</u> is past tense—use present tense <u>have</u>.
"friends [they] <u>leave</u> the party": You don't say "friends <u>to</u> leave the party."

2 The waves in the ocean <u>are</u> very high certain <u>times of the day</u>.

"The waves in the ocean [they] <u>are</u> very high": You don't say "[they] <u>is</u> very high." "certain <u>times</u> of the <u>day</u>."

3 Mrs. Martins was so angry at his brother and <u>him</u> that she took <u>their</u> allowances away that week.

"was so angry at his brother and [so angry at] <u>him</u>"

"she took <u>their</u> allowances": plural because of <u>his brother and him</u>

4 That's a <u>really</u> fast car that John and Paul <u>drive</u>.

"a <u>really</u> fast car": <u>really</u> modifies <u>fast</u>, the verb.

"that John and Paul [they] <u>drive</u>": You don't say they <u>drives</u>.

5 He would buy the toy if he <u>had</u> enough money.
"would buy . . . if he <u>had</u>"
This is the *subjunctive mood,* which indicates he didn't have enough money. "He would if he had" takes this form.

6 Harry and John will take <u>their</u> dog wherever they are <u>likely to go</u>.
"their" because of possession
"wherever they are likely to [they] <u>go</u>"

7 Where <u>there</u> is a will, there is a way.
"there is"

8 John <u>had</u> never been so scared <u>as</u> he was on Thursday night.
"John <u>had</u> never been" because of <u>past tense</u>.
Not "<u>like</u> he was" but "<u>as</u> he was."

9 George and Jim <u>are</u> very careful about not <u>spilling</u> anything.
"George and Jim [they] <u>are</u> very careful"
"about not <u>spilling</u> anything"

10 Last Friday, gobs of rain <u>poured</u> down the <u>windowsills</u>.

"gobs of rain [they] <u>poured</u> down"
"<u>windowsills</u>" not "<u>windows sill</u>"

11 All the kittens in the litter <u>were</u> for sale.

"kittens in the litter [they] <u>were</u> for sale"

TEN QUESTIONS ON ENGLISH EXPRESSION

Have your child answer the following questions. Go over your child's answers and compare them with the answers given following the question section. Then show your child how to correct his or her mistakes. You may want to explain to your child the directions to the questions.

Directions: In each of these sentences there may be an error in wording. If there is an error, choose the underlined part that should be changed in order to make the sentence correct. No sentence has more than one error, and some have none. If there is no error, choose D.

EXAMPLE

They <u>is</u> <u>coming</u> to the party tomorrow <u>night</u>. <u>No error</u>.
   A   B   C   D
Here you would Choose A, since the underlined word marked A is incorrect.

EXAMPLE

John and I <u>were</u> very happy when we <u>found</u> out <u>our</u> scores on
          A   B   C
the test. <u>No error</u>.
        D
Here you would choose D, since there is <u>no error</u>.

QUESTIONS

1 <u>Of</u> all my three brothers, John <u>is</u> the <u>worser</u> soccer player. <u>No</u>
   A   B   C

<u>error.</u>
 D

2 Sam dropped <u>his</u> money on the sidewalk; however, when he
          A

looked for it, he <u>couldn't</u> find it <u>nowhere.</u> <u>No error.</u>
             B   C   D

3 The coins <u>were</u> so strange <u>that</u> we couldn't decide where <u>it</u>
         A   B   C

came from. <u>No error.</u>
          D

4 You <u>will</u> not <u>only</u> see a beautiful sunset, <u>and</u> also see a
     A   B   C

gorgeous sunrise. <u>No error.</u>
             D

5 All people in <u>our</u> group <u>teaches</u> the members in the other
            A   B

groups <u>how</u> to cook. <u>No error.</u>
      C   D

6 The Martin family was so <u>likable</u> that we decided to give <u>it</u> a
                   A   B

box <u>of</u> cookies. <u>No error.</u>
    C   D

7 John was sure <u>that</u> he <u>has</u> arrived at school on time, but it
          A   B

<u>appeared</u> that he was late. <u>No error.</u>
  C   D

8 Some things <u>should be</u> read carefully, others less carefully, and
          A

<u>still</u> others <u>not at all.</u> <u>No error.</u>
 B   C   D

9 Everyone <u>in the</u> classroom <u>were</u> surprised to see a monkey
          A   B

<u>walk into</u> the room. <u>No error.</u>
  C   D

10 Paul and Sue <u>saw</u> <u>me and Jeffrey</u> <u>in</u> the classroom.
               A   B   C

<u>No error.</u>
 D

ANSWERS

1 (C) ". . . John is the <u>worst</u> soccer player."

2 (C) ". . . he couldn't find it <u>anywhere</u>."

3 (C) ". . . we couldn't decide where <u>they</u> came from" (<u>they</u> refers to <u>coins</u>).

4 (C) "You will not only see a beautiful sunset, <u>but</u> also see . . ."

5 (B) "All people in our group [they] <u>teach</u> . . ."

6 (B) ". . . we decided to give <u>them</u> [the Martin family] a box of cookies."

7 (B) "John was so sure that he <u>had</u> arrived at school on time . . ." Use <u>had</u> to indicate the past of <u>was</u>.

8 (D) No error.

9 (B) "Everyone in the classroom <u>was</u> surprised . . ." "Everyone . . . <u>was</u>"—was refers to <u>everyone</u> (singular).

10 (B) "Paul and Sue saw <u>Jeffrey and me</u> . . ." Always put the other person before *me, I, myself,* and so on.

Choosing the Right Word

The difference between the right word and the almost-right word is the difference between lightning and the lightning bug (firefly).

—Mark Twain

Here are a number of words that are commonly misused. You may want to look through this list yourself and then explain some of the misuses of words to your child. This list, however, is really for your reference so that you can check from time to time whether your child is misusing a word.

A, AN. The indefinite article *a* is used before a consonant sound; the indefinite article *an* is used before a vowel sound. Say *a plan, an idea.*

ACCEPT, EXCEPT. *Accept* means *to receive; except* when used as a verb means *to leave out.* (We *accepted* the gift. Pedro's name was *excepted* from the honor roll.) The word *except* is used most often as a preposition. *Everyone went except me.*

AFFECT, EFFECT. *Affect* is a verb that means to *influence.* (Winning the sweepstakes will *affect* his attitude.) *Effect,* as a noun, means *an influence.* (Smoking has an *effect* on one's health.) *Effect,* as a verb, means to *bring about.* (The teacher's praise *effected* a change in the student.)

Affected, as an adjective, has the meaning of *false.* (She had an *affected* way of speaking.)

AGGRAVATE, IRRITATE. *Aggravate* means to make worse. (Drinking ice water will *aggravate* your cold.) *Irritate* means to *annoy* or *exasperate.* (Mary's continuous chattering *irritated* me.)

AIN'T. Do not use this expression.

ALREADY, ALL READY. *Already* means *before* or *by a certain time.* (Mike said that he had *already* done the job.) *All ready* means *completely ready.* (When the buzzer sounded, the horses were *all ready* to start running.)

ALL RIGHT, ALRIGHT. The only correct spelling is *all right.*

ALTOGETHER, ALL TOGETHER. *Altogether* means *entirely, wholly.* (Jane is *altogether* too conceited to get along with people.) *All together* means *as a group.* (After the explosion, the boss was relieved to find his workers *all together* in front of the building.)

AMONG, BETWEEN. *Among* is used with more than two persons or things. (The manager distributed the gifts *among* all of the employed.) *Between* is used only with two persons or things. (The steak was divided *between the two children.*)

AMOUNT, NUMBER. *Amount* is used to refer to things in bulk. (The war costs a great *amount* of money.) *Number* is used to refer to things that can be counted. (A large *number* of pupils attend this school.)

AND ETC. This is incorrect. The abbreviation *etc.* stands for the Latin *et cetera.* The *et* means *and;* the *cetera* means *other things.* It is wrong to say *and etc.* because the idea of *and* is already included in the *etc.*

ANYWAYS, ANYWHERES, EVERYWHERES, SOMEWHERES. These expressions are not correct. Omit the final *s* after each.

AS, LIKE. *As,* used as a conjunction, is followed by a verb. (Please do it *as* I told you to.) *Like* may not be used as a conjunction. If it is used as a preposition, it is not followed by a verb. (This ice cream looks *like* custard.)

AWFUL. See **TERRIFIC, TERRIBLE.**

BEING THAT. *Being that* is incorrect when used to mean *since* or *because.* (*Since* you are tired, you ought to rest.)

BESIDE, BESIDES. *Beside* means *alongside of; besides* means *in addition to.* (Nixon sat *beside* Autry at the baseball game.) (There is nobody *besides* her husband who understands Ann.)

BETWEEN. See **AMONG.**

BRING, TAKE. Consider the speaker as a starting point. *Bring* is used for something carried in the direction of the speaker. (When you return from lunch, please *bring* me a ham sandwich.) *Take* is used for something carried away from the speaker. (If you are going downtown, please *take* this letter to the post office.)

BUNCH. *Bunch* means cluster. Do no use *bunch* for group or crowd. (This is a large *bunch* of grapes.) (A *crowd* of people were at the scene of the accident.)

BUT THAT, BUT WHAT. Do not use these expressions in place of *that* in structures like the following: I do not question *that* (not *but that*) you are richer than I am.

CAN'T HARDLY. Don't use this double negative. Say *can hardly.*

CONTINUAL, CONTINUOUS. *Continual* means happening at intervals. (Salespeople are *continually* walking into this office.) *Continuous* means going on without interruption. (Without a moment of dry weather, it rained *continuously* for forty days and forty nights.)

COULD OF. Do not use to mean *could have.*

DATA. Although *data* is the plural of *datum,* idiom permits the use of this word as a singular. Some authorities still insist on *Data are gathered* rather than *Data is gathered* or *these data* rather than *this data.* Most people in computer programming now say *Data is gathered* or *this data.*

DEAL. Do not use this term for *arrangement* or *transaction.* (He has an *excellent arrangement* (not *deal*) with the manager.)

DIFFERENT FROM, DIFFERENT THAN. *Different from* is correct. *Different than* is incorrect. (His method of doing this is *different from* mine.)

DISCOVER, INVENT. *Discover* means to see or learn something that has not been previously known. (They say the Vikings, not Columbus, *discovered* America.) *Invent* means to create for the first time. (William S. Burroughs *invented* the adding machine.)

DISINTERESTED, UNINTERESTED. *Disinterested* means without bias. (An umpire must be *disinterested* to judge fairly in a baseball game.) *Uninterested* means not caring about a situation. (I am totally *uninterested* in your plan.)

DOESN'T, DON'T. *Doesn't* means *does not; don't* means *do not.* Do not say *He don't (do not)* when you mean *He doesn't (does not).*

DUE TO. At the beginning of a sentence, *due to* is always incorrect. Use, instead, *on account of, because of,* or a similar expression. (*On account of* bad weather, the contest was postponed.) As a predicate adjective construction, *due to* is correct. His weakness was *due to* his hunger.

EACH OTHER, ONE ANOTHER. *Each other* is used for two persons. (The executive and his secretary antagonize *each other.*) *One another* is used for more than two persons. The members of the large family love *one another.*)

EFFECT. See **AFFECT.**

ENTHUSE. Do not use this word. Say *enthusiastic.* (The art critic was *enthusiastic* about the painting.)

EQUALLY AS GOOD. This expression is incorrect. Say, instead, *just as good.* (This car is *just as good* as that.)

FARTHER, FURTHER. *Farther* is used for a distance that is measurable. (The farmer's house is about 100 yards *farther* down the road.) *Further* is used to express the extension of an idea. (A *further* explanation may be necessary.)

FEWER, LESS. *Fewer* applies to what may be counted. (Greenwich Village has *fewer* conservatives than liberals.) *Less* refers to degree or amount. (*Less* rain fell this month than the month before.)

FLOUT, FLAUNT. *Flout* means to mock or insult. (The king *flouted* the wise man when the latter offered advice.) *Flaunt* means to make a pretentious display of. (The upstart *flaunted* his diamond ring.)

FURTHER. See **FARTHER.**

GET. *Get* means *to obtain* or *receive.* Get should not be used in the sense of *to excite, to interest,* or *to understand.* Say: His guitar playing *fascinates* (not *gets*) me. Say: When you talk about lifestyles, I just don't *understand* (not *get*) you.

GOOD, WELL. Do not use the adjective *good* in place of the adverb *well* in structures like the following: John works *well* (not *good*) in the kitchen. Jim pitched *well* (not *good*) in last night's game.

GRADUATE. One *graduates from,* or *is graduated from,* a school. One does *not graduate a school.* (The student *graduated* [or *was graduated*] from high school.)

HAD OF. Avoid using this to mean *had.* Say: My father always said that he wished he *had* (not *had of*) gone to college.

HANGED, HUNG. When a person is *executed,* he or she is *hanged.* When anything is *suspended* in space, it is *hung.*

HARDLY. See **CAN'T HARDLY.**

HEALTHFUL, HEALTHY. *Healthful* applies to *conditions that promote health. Healthy* applies to *a state of health.* Say: Stevenson found the climate of Saranac Lakes very *healthful.* Say: Mary is a very *healthy* girl.

IF, WHETHER. Use *whether*—not *if*—in structures that follow verbs like *ask, doubt, know, learn, say.* Say: Hank Aaron didn't know *whether* (not *if*) he was going to break Babe Ruth's homerun record.

IMPLY, INFER. The speaker *implies* when he suggests or hints at. (The owner of the store *implied* that the patron stole a box of toothpicks.) The listener *infers* when he draws a conclusion from facts or evidence. (From what you say, I *infer* that I am about to be discharged.)

IN, INTO. *In* is used to express a location, without the involvement of motion. (The sugar is *in* the cupboard.) *Into* is used to express motion from one place to another. (The housekeeper put the sugar *into* the cupboard.)

IN REGARDS TO. This is incorrect. Say *in regard to* or *with regard to.*

INVENT. See **DISCOVER.**

IRREGARDLESS. Do not use *irregardless.* It is incorrect for *regardless.* (You will not be able to go out tonight *regardless* of the fact that you have done all of your homework.)

ITS, IT'S. *Its* is the possessive of *it; it's* is the contraction for *it is.*

KIND OF, SORT OF. Do not use these expressions as adverbs. Say: Ali was *quite* (not *kind of* or *sort of*) witty in his post-fight interview.

KIND OF A, SORT OF A. Omit the *a*. Say: What *kind of* (not *kind of a* or *sort of a*) game is lacrosse?

LEARN, TEACH. *Learn* means *gaining knowledge. Teach* means *imparting knowledge.* Say: He *taught* (not *learned*) his brother how to swim.

LEAVE, LET. The word *leave* means *to depart.* (I *leave* today for San Francisco.) The word *let* means to allow. (*Let* me take your place.)

LESS, FEWER. See **FEWER, LESS.**

LIABLE, LIKELY. *Liable* means exposed to something unpleasant. (If you speed, you are *liable* to get a summons.) *Likely* means probable, with reference to either a pleasant or unpleasant happening. (It is *likely* to snow tomorrow.)

LOCATE. Do not use *locate* to mean *settle* or *move to.* Say: We will *move to* (not *locate in*) Florida next year.

MIGHT OF, MUST OF. Omit the *of.* We *might have* or *must have.*

MYSELF, HIMSELF, YOURSELF. These pronouns are to be used as intensives. (The chairman *himself* will open the meeting.) Do not use these pronouns when *me, him,* or *you* will serve. Say: We shall be happy if Joe and *you* (not *yourself*) join us for lunch at the Plaza.

NICE. See **TERRIFIC, TERRIBLE.**

NUMBER, AMOUNT. See **AMOUNT, NUMBER.**

OF, HAVE. Do not use *of* for *have* in structures like *could have.*

OFF OF. Omit the *of.* Say: The book fell *off* (not *off of*) the shelf.

POUR, SPILL. When one *pours,* he or she does it deliberately. (He carefully *poured* the wine into her glass.) When one *spills,* he or she does it accidentally. (I carelessly *spilled* some wine on her dress.)

PRACTICAL, PRACTICABLE. *Practical* means *fitted for actual work. Practicable* means *feasible* or *possible.* Say: My business partner is a *practical* man. Say: The boss did not consider the plan *practicable* for this coming year.

PRINCIPAL, PRINCIPLE. *Principal* applies to a *chief* or the *chief part* of something. *Principle* applies to a *basic law.* Say: Mr. Jones is the *principal* of the school. Professor White was the *principal* speaker. Honesty is a good *principle* to follow.

REASON IS BECAUSE. Do not use the expression *reason is because*—it is always incorrect. Say the *reason is that.* (The *reason* Jack failed the course *is that* he didn't study.)

REGARDLESS. See **IRREGARDLESS.**

RESPECTFULLY, RESPECTIVELY. *Respectfully* means *with respect* as in the complimentary close of a letter, *respectfully yours. Respectively* means that each item will be considered *in the order given.* Say: This paper is *respectfully* submitted. Say: The hero, the heroine, and the villain will be played by Albert, Joan, and Harry *respectively.*

SAID. Avoid such legalistic uses of *said* as *said letter, said plan, said program,* except in legal writing.

SHOULD OF. Do not use to mean *should have.*

SOME. Do not use *some* when you mean *somewhat.* Say: I'm *somewhat* (not *some*) confused.

SPILL, POUR. See **POUR, SPILL.**

SUSPICION. Do not use *suspicion* as a verb when you mean *suspect.*

TAKE, BRING. See **BRING, TAKE.**

TEACH, LEARN. See **LEARN, TEACH.**

TERRIFIC, TERRIBLE. Avoid "lazy words." Many people don't want to take the trouble to use the exact word. They will use words like *terrific, swell, great, beautiful,* and so on to describe anything and everything that is favorable. And they will use words like *terrible, awful, lousy, and miserable,* for whatever is unfavorable. Use the exact word. Say: We had a *delicious* (not terrific) meal. Say: We had a *boring* (not *terrible*) *weekend.*

THIS KIND, THESE KIND. *This kind* is correct—as is *that kind, these kinds,* and *those kinds.* (My little brother likes *this kind* of pears.) *These kind* and *those kind* are incorrect.

TRY AND. Do not say *try and.* Say *try to.* (*Try to* visit me while I am in Florida.)

UNINTERESTED. See **DISINTERESTED.**

WAIT FOR, WAIT ON. *Wait for* means *to await; wait on* means *to serve.* Say: I am waiting *for* (not *on*) Carter to call me on the telephone.

WAY, WAYS. Do not use *ways* for *way.* Say: It is a long *way* (not *ways*) to Japan.

WHERE. Do not use *where* in place of *that* in expressions like the following: I see in the newspaper *that* (not *where*) a nuclear reactor may be built a mile away from our house.

WOULD OF. Do not use to mean *would have.*

MATH STRATEGIES

A Note to Parents

In this chapter, you and your child will be presented with various strategies and critical-thinking skills to be used in solving math problems. If as you go along you begin to feel that your child is lacking certain basic information in an area of math such as geometry, refer to the section entitled "Math Words, Concepts and Rules Your Child Should Know," on pages 113-124. Your child can also look at "Math Shortcuts Your Child Should Know," on pages 125-134. Finally, if you feel that your child should brush up on his or her basics *before* beginning to learn the strategies, have a look at "The Fifty Basic Math Problems for Grades 3 • 4 • 5," on pages 135-147. You may want to have your child work on these before he or she begins to study the strategies.

Before beginning to work on the math strategies presented in this part of the book, you should also review the four-step learning method described in the "Introduction to Parents," on page 1.

BASIC MATH STRATEGIES

The six strategies presented below will help your child to answer math questions more quickly and accurately by enabling your child to: first, focus his or her mind on each problem in the most appropriate way, and second, use a variety of strategic shortcuts in working out the solutions to problems.

MATH STRATEGY 1:
Know How to Approach Solutions to Math Questions

One of the most important things to know in answering any math question is how to *start* the solution. So many students rush into a solution without taking the time to think about what the question is really asking or aiming at.

The key to solving math questions is knowing *how to extract from the question the useful pieces of information* that will enable your child to solve it.

Once the student can see pieces of information that *contain something useful,* he or she develops confidence, which helps him or her proceed to the solution of the question.

Here are some examples:

EXAMPLE 1

How would it be best to measure the distance between New York and California?

  (A) in meters
  (B) in centimeters
  (C) in millimeters
  (D) in kilometers

Think about what piece or pieces of information can be extracted from this question that will be useful in finding a solution. We know that the distance between New York and California is some *large* number. So we want to look for a choice that contains a *large* number. A kilometer is 1,000 meters, so Choice D is correct.

EXAMPLE 2

Sam receives twice as much money as Bill. If Sam receives $1.40, how much does Bill get?

(A) $2.80
(B) $.70
(C) $2.40
(D) $.50

What can be extracted from this question that gives the most useful information?

1 Sam receives $1.40.

2 Sam receives twice as much as Bill.

So, what can we readily calculate?
Since Sam receives *twice* as much as Bill and Sam gets $1.40, Bill must get one half of $1.40, or $.70. Choice B is correct.

EXAMPLE 3

$7 + \Box = 15$. Which gives the number $\Box$?

(A) $7 + 15$
(B) $7 - 15$
(C) $15 - 7$
(D) 15×7

What piece of information is given? $7 + \Box = 15$.
What is it necessary to find? What $\Box$ is equal to.
So what must be done? We have to *isolate* the $\Box$ in the equation $7 + \Box = 15$, so that $\Box$ is alone.
How can we do this? We get rid of the 7 on the left side of the equation by *subtracting* 7 from both sides of the equal-sign:

$$7 + \Box = 15$$
$$-7 \qquad = -7$$
$$\overline{7 + \Box - 7 = 15 - 7} \quad \text{(answer)}$$
$$\text{So} \qquad \Box = 15 - 7$$

Choice C is correct.

Sometimes all the information given in a problem is not needed. So, what is really needed for immediate solution has to be *extracted*. The following is a good example of this kind of question.

EXAMPLE 4

Sarah is 9 years old. She made 5 pies in 3 hours. She was able to sell these pies for $1 each. Which describes how much she got for the pies?

    (A) $9 \times \$1$
    (B) $3 \times \$1$
    (C) $(5 \times 3) \times \$1$
    (D) $5 \times \$1$

A lot of information is given here that is not needed to solve the problem. So we have to extract what is needed. How do we do this? Since we want to find out "how much she got for the pies," we are really looking for *how much she gets for each pie* and *how many pies she sells.* The question says she sold 5 pies at $1 each. So $5 \times \$1$ would give the amount she got for all the pies. It isn't necessary to use the fact that she was 9 years old or that it took her 3 hours to make the pies. Choice D is correct.

So in summary, your child should:

1 Know what he or she is being asked to find.

2 Try to extract the pieces of information that will be useful for solution.

After you have gone over the previous examples with your child, have him or her try the following exercises.

QUESTIONS

1 Chet bought 4 packages of doughnuts. There were 5 doughnuts in each package. He also bought 3 packages of doughnuts with 7 doughnuts in each package. How many doughnuts did he buy?
    (A) 19
    (B) 7
    (C) 12
    (D) 41

2 Paul owes Sandy $1.50. If Paul gives Sandy $.80, how much does he now owe Sandy?
    (A) $1.30
    (B) $.70
    (C) $.80
    (D) $.90

3 $18 - \square = 10$. Which gives the number $\square$?

    (A) $18 - 10$

    (B) $10 - 18$

    (C) $18 + 10$

    (D) $10 + 18$

4 Harry mixed $\dfrac{1}{2}$ cup of yellow paint with some red paint to make $\dfrac{3}{4}$ cup of orange paint. How much red paint did Harry use?

    (A) $\dfrac{5}{4}$ cup

    (B) $\dfrac{1}{4}$ cup

    (C) $\dfrac{2}{3}$ cup

    (D) $\dfrac{6}{4}$ cup

SOLUTIONS

1 (D) You want to find out *how many doughnuts*. So you need to know the number of doughnuts in each package, and multiply this by the number of packages.

Chet bought 4 packages of doughnuts—each package contained 5 doughnuts. So there were

$4 \times 5 = 20$ doughnuts in the first set of packages.

He also bought 3 packages of doughnuts—each package contained 7 doughnuts. So there were

$3 \times 7 = 21$ doughnuts in the second set of packages.

The number of doughnuts is:

$21 + 20 = 41$.

2 (B) What is given? <u>Paul owes Sandy $1.50</u>, and <u>Paul gave Sandy $.80.</u>

So what can be extracted from this information? Since Paul gave Sandy $.80, he only owes Sandy:

$$\$1.50 - \$.80 = \$.70$$

3 (A) You are given

$$18 - \square = 10.$$

You want to find $\square$, so you want to get $\square$ alone.
How do we do this?
Add to both sides of the equal-sign to get rid of the minus sign:

$$18 - \square = 10$$
$$+ \qquad \square = \square$$
$$\overline{18 - \cancel{\square} + \cancel{\square} = 10 + \square}$$

we get $18 = 10 + \square$

Now subtract 10 from both sides of the equal-sign to get $\square$ alone:

$$18 = 10 + \square$$
$$- 10 = 10$$
$$\overline{18 - 10 = \cancel{10} + \square - \cancel{10}}$$

or $18 - 10 = \square$

4 (B) You are given that 1/2 cup of yellow paint and some red paint make 3/4 cup of orange paint. Let $\square$ be the cups of red paint.

$$\text{So, } \frac{1}{2} + \square = \frac{3}{4}$$

You want to find $\square$

Subtract $\dfrac{1}{2}$ from both sides of equal-sign to get $\square$ alone.

$$\frac{1}{2} + \square = \frac{3}{4}$$

$$- \qquad \frac{1}{2} = \frac{1}{2}$$

$$\overline{\frac{\cancel{1}}{\cancel{2}} - \frac{\cancel{1}}{\cancel{2}} + \square = \frac{3}{4} - \frac{1}{2}}$$

$$\square = \frac{3}{4} - \frac{1}{2}$$

Remember or learn the shortcut for subtracting fractions (see page 126):

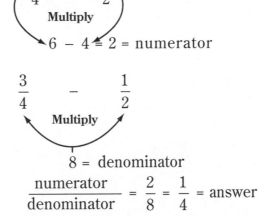

$$6 - 4 = 2 = \text{numerator}$$

$$\frac{3}{4} \qquad - \qquad \frac{1}{2}$$

$$8 = \text{denominator}$$

$$\frac{\text{numerator}}{\text{denominator}} = \frac{2}{8} = \frac{1}{4} = \text{answer}$$

MATH STRATEGY 2: Use Math Symbols for Words

Math problems expressed in nonmathematical terms are the most difficult kinds of math questions. If your child does not know the right strategy, he or she could become exhausted trying to do some of these brain-racking problems. However, there is a strategy that can make these problems much simpler: substituting math symbols for words.

As early as possible, you should familiarize your child with math symbols, so that he or she can use them as a shortcut in solving those kinds of problems that are expressed mostly in words. Here's an example:

EXAMPLE 1

Harry had 64 crayons and lost 5 of them. How many crayons did he have left?

(A) 59
(B) 60
(C) 69
(D) 79

The word <u>lost</u> should be translated to – (minus). So:

$$64 \quad \text{lost} \quad 5$$

$$\text{becomes} \quad \downarrow \quad \downarrow \quad \downarrow$$

$$64 \quad - \quad 5$$

This is equal to 59. (Choice A).

The table below will help in changing words into math symbols. Your child should gradually become familiar with this table.

Word	Equivalent Math Symbol	Equivalent Word	Math Symbol
and	+	of	$\times$
added to	+	twice as many	$2\times$
gave	+	half as many	$\frac{1}{2}\times$
got	+	percent	$\overline{100}$
gained greater than	+ +	increased 20 percent	$+\ \dfrac{20}{100}\times$ original * value
has, had	+	reduced 20 percent	$-\ \dfrac{20}{100}\times$ original * value
increased by	+	are, is, was	=
received	+	equal to	=
sum of	+	has, had	=
* m years from now	$+m$	same as	=
decreased by	–	less than	<
difference of	–	shorter than	<
less	–	younger than	<
lost	–	greater than	>
owe	–	older than	>
subtract from	–	taller than	>
* m years ago	$-m$	John, Phil, Sam, etc.	J, P, S, etc.
		What	? or □ , etc.
		what (or any unknown)	x, n, N, etc. *

* is for the advanced child

Note: *If $a > b$, and $b > c$, then $a > c$.
　　　*$a > b$ is the same as $b < a$.
　　　*$b > c$ is the same as $c < b$.
　　　*$a > c$ is the same as $c < a$.

Let's try two more examples using the above table.

EXAMPLE 2

Phil is shorter than Mary but taller than John. Which of the three is tallest?

    (A) Phil
    (B) Mary
    (C) John
    (D) cannot tell

Here's the solution (with the translation):

Phil is shorter than Mary.
   ↓   ↓   ↓
   P   <   M

But Phil is taller than John.
   ↓   ↓   ↓
   P   >   J

So $P < M$ and $P > J$.

Write $M > P$ (this means the same as $P < M$).
So we have: $M > P$ and $P > J$.

We can now see that M must be greater than J ($M > J$). Since M is also $> P$, therefore M is tallest (Choice B).

EXAMPLE 3

Five sixths of thirty is what?

    (A) 20
    (B) 25
    (C) 30
    (D) 15

Translate the question to math symbols, as shown below. Remember that <u>of</u> becomes × and <u>is</u> becomes =.

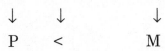

Five sixths of thirty is what?
   ↓   ↓ ↓ ↓ ↓
$$\frac{5}{6} \times 30 = ?$$

$$\frac{5}{\cancel{6}} \times \overset{5}{\cancel{30}} = 25 \quad \text{(Choice B)}.$$

Now have your child try these exercises:

1 John had 103 marbles and lost 4 of them. How many does he have now?
(A) 99 (B) 107 (C) 110 (D) 112

2 Mary had $3 on Monday. John gave her $2 the next day, Tuesday, and Paul gave Mary $1 on Wednesday. How much does Mary have after Wednesday?
(A) $1 (B) $2 (C) $5 (D) $6

3 Sam is older than Paul but younger than Harry. Who is oldest?
(A) Sam (B) Paul (C) Harry (D) cannot tell

4 John has $5 but owes Mary and Sue $2 each. If he pays Mary and Sue, how much does he have left?
(A) $1 (B) $2 (C) $3 (D) $4

5 What is 20 percent of 200?
(A) 400 (B) 40 (C) 4 (D) 4,000

SOLUTIONS

1 (A) <u>Lost</u> means – so we get:

103 lost 4

↓ ↓ ↓

103 – 4

Use the short cut:

$$103 - 4 = \underbrace{103 - 100}_{} + \underbrace{100 - 4}_{}$$

$$= \quad 3 \quad + \quad 96$$
$$= \quad 99$$

2 (D) <u>Has</u> in math terms means +.
<u>Gives</u> in math terms means +.

Mary   had $\underbrace{\$3}_{+3}$ John gives $\underbrace{\$2}_{+2}$ Paul gives $\underbrace{\$1}_{+1}$

3 + 2 + 1 = 6 (Choice D)

3 (C) Sam is <u>older</u> than Paul—<u>older</u> becomes the symbol >.

Sam is older than Paul.

↓   ↓   ↓

S   >   P

Sam is <u>younger</u> than Harry.

↓   ↓   ↓

S   <   H

(Note: <u>younger</u> becomes the symbol <.)

So we get:
S > P and H > S
(Note: H > S is the same as S < H.)
You can see that H > P (H is older than P) since H > S and S > P. Since H is also older than S (H > S), H is oldest. Choice C is correct.

4 (A) Translate as follows:

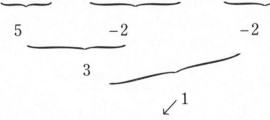

John has $5 but owes Mary $2 and owes Sue $2.

5   −2   −2

3

1

The answer is 1 (Choice A).

5 (B) Translate verbal to math. Remember, <u>percent</u> is $\frac{}{100}$, <u>is</u> becomes = and <u>of</u> becomes ×.

What is 20 percent of 200?

↓ ↓↓   ↓   ↓ ↓

? = 20 $\overline{100}$ × 200

$? = \dfrac{20}{100} \times 200$

$? = \dfrac{20}{\cancel{100}} \times \cancel{200}$

$? = 20 \times 2 = 40$ (Choice B).

MATH STRATEGY 3:
Know When and How to Approximate

Many times your child will encounter a question that asks not for an exact answer but for an *approximation* to an answer. At other times your child may want to approximate to find an answer more rapidly. So it is important to know how and when to approximate.

The following examples show typical problems where this strategy should be used.

EXAMPLE 1

Find:

$$\begin{array}{r} 7.6 \\ \times\, 9.9 \\ \hline \end{array}$$

    (A) 7,524
    (B) 752.4
    (C) 75.24
    (D) 7.524

This is a very easy question if one knows how to approximate. First let's look at the choices. There's quite a range in value there. So let's approximate 7.6 by 8 and 9.9 by 10. Now, multiply:

$$\begin{array}{r} 8 \\ \times\, 10 \\ \hline 80 \end{array}$$

The closest choice to 80 is Choice C, 75.24. Choice C is correct.

EXAMPLE 2

994 – 212 is closest to

    (A) 600
    (B) 700
    (C) 800
    (D) 900

Look at the choices first. They all end in hundreds (00). So approximate 994 by 1,000; that's the closest number ending in 00. And approximate 212 by 200, which is the closest number ending in 00.

So now we have to find: 1,000 – 200.
That's 800, which is Choice C.

EXAMPLE 3

What is 89,806 to the nearest thousand?

    (A) 89,000
    (B) 90,000
    (C) 89,900
    (D) 91,000

Here we have to read the question carefully to know what it asks for. We want to find 89,806 to the nearest thousand. What does that mean? It means we want a number as close to 89,806 but ending in 000 (thousand). It's either 90,000 or 89,000. But 90,000 is closer to 89,806, so Choice B is correct.

EXAMPLE 4

Which is closest to 91 + 78?

    (A) 90 + 70
    (B) 92 + 70
    (C) 90 + 80
    (D) 100 + 70

Look at the choices. We want a number close to 91 and a number close to 78. A number close to 91 is 90. A number close to 78 is 80.
    So, 90 + 80 must be the answer. Choice C is correct.

EXAMPLE 5

Which is about 4?

    (A) $20\overline{)480}$

    (B) $120\overline{)485}$

    (C) $120\overline{)4,800}$

    (D) $12\overline{)485}$

If we make the 5 in Choices B and D a 0, we won't change the answer by much. So the choices become:

    (A) $20\overline{)480}$ = $2\cancel{0}\overline{)48\cancel{0}}$ = 24

    (B) $120\overline{)480}$ = $12\cancel{0}\overline{)48\cancel{0}}$ = 4

    (C) $120\overline{)4,800}$ = $12\cancel{0}\overline{)480\cancel{0}}$ = 40

    (D) $12\overline{)480}$ = 40

Choice B is correct.
    Have him or her try the following exercises. After you have shown your child the preceding examples, check his or her solutions with the correct answers found after the questions.

QUESTIONS

1 What is 8.1 × 8.8?
  (A) 7,128
  (B) 712.8
  (C) 71.28
  (D) 7.128

2 1,001 − 194 = □. □ is closest to
  (A) 600
  (B) 700
  (C) 800
  (D) 900

3 What is 91,206 to the nearest hundred?
  (A) 91,100
  (B) 91,200
  (C) 90,200
  (D) 91,300

4 Which is closest to 89 + 81?
  (A) 100 + 90
  (B) 80 + 80
  (C) 90 + 90
  (D) 90 + 80

5 Which is about 3?

  (A) $40\overline{)1,200}$

  (B) $4\overline{)120}$

  (C) $400\overline{)1,220}$

  (D) $4\overline{)122}$

SOLUTIONS

1 (C) Look at the choices. There's quite a range. So we can be pretty safe by approximating 8.1 by 8 and 8.8 by 9. This produces:

$$\begin{array}{r} 8 \\ \times\ 9 \\ \hline 72 \end{array}$$

The closest answer is Choice C (71.28).

2 (C) Look at the choices. They all end in 00. So approximate 1,001 as 1,000. And approximate 194 as 200. Now subtract: 1,000 − 200 = 800. (Choice C).

3 (B) Read this carefully. It asks us to find 91,206 to the nearest hundred. So we're looking for a number ending in 00, not necessarily 000. The choices are 91,100, 91,200, 90,200, and 91,300; 91,206 to the nearest hundred is 91,200, since 206 is closer to 200 than to 300 or 100. Choice B is correct.

4 (D) Look at the choices. Look for a number close to 89 and a number close to 81: 90 is close to 89 and 80 is close to 81. So the number closest to 89 + 81 is 90 + 80 (choice D).

5 (C) Simplify by letting the 1,220 in Choice C be 1,200, and the 122 in Choice D be 120. This makes it more comparable with the other choices. So the choices become:

(A) $40\overline{)1,200} = 4\not0\overline{)1,20\not0} = 30$

(B) $4\overline{)120} = 30$

(C) $400\overline{)1,200} = 4\not0\not0\overline{)1,2\not0\not0} = 3$

(D) $4\overline{)120} = 30$

Choice C is correct.

MATH STRATEGY 4:
Try Specific Numbers

Many math questions become much clearer when numbers are put into the problem. By doing this, your child will gain confidence, because numbers are something concrete, and working with them makes students feel like they are moving toward a solution.

Here are some good examples:

EXAMPLE 1

An odd number subtracted from an odd number is

(A) an odd number
(B) an even number
(C) 0
(D) not determined as being odd or even

Choose any two odd numbers (simple ones, so that things don't become complicated). Like 1 and 3.

$$3 - 1 = 2$$

Lo and behold, we get an even number. Now try another set of odd numbers. Like 3 and 5.

$$5 - 3 = 2$$

An even number again!

I'd choose Choice B at this point. But if you're still not sure, try again with two more odd numbers.

EXAMPLE 2

Sam is taller than John. John is taller than Phil. Which of the three boys is shortest?

(A) Sam
(B) John
(C) Phil
(D) cannot tell

You could of course use Strategy 2 (verbal-to-math symbols) here. But let's see how to do this when you plug in numbers.
Let Sam be 60 inches tall.
Now Sam is taller than John, so let John be 55 inches.
John is taller than Phil. So let Phil be 51 inches.
You can see that Phil is shortest. Choice C is correct.

EXAMPLE 3

An even number plus 3 is always a number that is

(A) even
(B) odd
(C) a multiple of 3
(D) greater than 5

Choose a simple even number. Like 2. An even number plus 3 becomes $2 + 3$.
$2 + 3 = 5$. Choice B is correct.
If you're still not sure, just eliminate the other choices:

Choice A: The number is not always even because 5 is a possibility that is odd.

Choice C: It is not always a multiple of 3 since 5 is not a multiple of 3.

Choice D: It is not always greater than 5 since one possibility *is* 5.

The only choice left is Choice B.

EXAMPLE 4

Harry wrapped $\frac{1}{6}$ of the boxes and John wrapped $\frac{5}{12}$ of the boxes.
What fraction of the boxes did both Harry and John wrap?

(A) $\frac{7}{12}$

(B) $\frac{1}{2}$

(C) $\frac{3}{5}$

(D) $\frac{5}{6}$

This is a good example of using numbers in a problem. Let the total number of boxes be a multiple of 12—you'll realize why this is a good number to use as we work out the problem. Let the total number of boxes be 12—the simplest multiple of 12.

Harry wrapped $\dfrac{1}{6}$ of the boxes so he wrapped $\dfrac{1}{6}$ of 12 boxes.

$$\frac{1}{6} \text{ of } 12 = \frac{1}{6} \times 12 = \underline{2 \text{ boxes}} \text{ (for Harry)}$$

John wrapped $\dfrac{5}{12}$ of the boxes so he wrapped $\dfrac{5}{12}$ of 12 boxes.

$$\frac{5}{12} \text{ of } 12 \text{ boxes} = \frac{5}{12} \times 12 = \underline{5 \text{ boxes}} \text{ (for John)}$$

So both Harry and John wrapped $\underline{2 + 5} = \underline{7}$ boxes.
The total number of boxes is $\underline{12,}$ so the fraction that both Harry and John wrapped is:

$$\frac{\text{Part} \rightarrow}{\text{Total} \rightarrow} \frac{7}{12} \text{(Choice A)}$$

After you have shown your child the previous strategy and questions, have him or her try the following exercises.

QUESTIONS

1 An even number subtracted from an even number is
   - (A) even
   - (B) odd
   - (C) 0
   - (D) not defined as being odd or even

2 Harry is older than Sue. Amy is younger than Sue. Who is oldest?
   - (A) Harry
   - (B) Sue
   - (C) Amy
   - (D) cannot tell

3 An odd number plus 2 is always
   - (A) even
   - (B) odd
   - (C) greater than 3
   - (D) a multiple of 2

4 Mary used $\dfrac{1}{6}$ of the blackboard for her drawing. Sam used $\dfrac{1}{3}$ of the blackboard for his drawing. What fraction of the blackboard did both Mary and Sam use?
   - (A) $\dfrac{1}{2}$
   - (B) $\dfrac{1}{4}$
   - (C) $\dfrac{2}{5}$
   - (D) $\dfrac{2}{3}$

SOLUTIONS

1 (A) Try specific numbers. Let the even numbers be 2 and 4. Remember to always choose the simplest numbers so that you don't make things unnecessarily difficult.

An even number subtracted from an even number:

$$\textbf{Even} \searrow \quad \nearrow \textbf{Even}$$
$$4 - 2 = 2$$
$$\searrow \textbf{Even}$$

The answer is an even number. Choice A is correct.

2 (A) Let Harry be 12 years old. Since Harry is older than Sue, let Sue be 10 years old. Amy is younger than Sue so let Amy be 9 years old. The oldest is Harry. Choice A is correct.

3 (B) Let the odd number be 1 (that's the simplest odd number).
An odd number plus 2 is $1 + 2$

$$\textbf{Odd} \rightarrow 1 + 2 = 3, \text{ which is odd.}$$

Choice B is correct.

4 (A) Let the whole blackboard have 6 parts: 6 is the simplest multiple of 6 which is in the $\frac{1}{6}$ that Mary used. You'll realize why 6 was chosen as you work out the problem.

Mary used $\frac{1}{6}$ and there are 6 parts, so Mary used $\frac{1}{6} \times 6 =$ 1 part.

Sam used $\frac{1}{3}$ and there are 6 parts, so Sam used $\frac{1}{3} \times 6 =$ 2 parts.

So both Mary and Sam used $1 + 2 = 3$ parts.
The total number of parts is 6, so the fraction of the blackboard that both Mary and Sam used is:

$$\frac{\text{Part} \rightarrow 3}{\text{Total} \rightarrow 6} = \frac{1}{2}$$

Choice A is correct.

MATH STRATEGY 5: Start with Last Choice When Testing Choices

The test designer is a very clever person. The test maker expects that if your child has to try all the choices to see which one is correct, your child will start with Choice A. In order to weed out poor students, the test maker hopes that if your child doesn't know how to solve a problem, he or she will make a mistake *before* getting to the *right choice.* So for this particular type of question the test maker usually puts the right choice at the end of the string of choices: C or D (or D or E if there is an E choice). Thus, by the time your child gets to the right choice, he or she will usually have eliminated two or three of the incorrect ones. So here's a useful strategy for four-choice questions: *Always start with Choice D* and *then go to C, B, and A.* (For five-choice questions, start with Choice E.)

Practice using this strategy in the following examples.

EXAMPLE 1

Which is equal to 6?

(A) 3×3
(B) 2×4
(C) 6×0
(D) 6×1

Here you have to really try the choices. Start with Choice D: 6×1. That's 6, so you got your answer *without having to look at the other choices!*

EXAMPLE 2

Which is correct?

(A) $86 > 89$
(B) $95 > 101$
(C) $102 > 103$
(D) $320 > 289$

Again you have to test the choices. Start with Choice D: $320 > 289$. That's the answer. Again you got the right answer *without having to even look at the other choices!*

EXAMPLE 3

Which figure always has sides that meet at right angles?

(A) a triangle
(B) a circle
(C) a rectangle
(D) a parallelogram

Start with Choice D: A parallelogram does not have sides that meet at right angles:

Go on to Choice C: A rectangle does have sides that meet at right angles.

Choice C is correct.

EXAMPLE 4

Which is <u>not</u> true?

(A) $\dfrac{3}{3} = \dfrac{1}{1}$

(B) $\dfrac{5}{5} = \dfrac{4}{4}$

(C) $\dfrac{3}{5} = \dfrac{5}{3}$

(D) $\dfrac{6}{6} = 1$

You have to test the choices, so start with the last one, Choice D: $\dfrac{6}{6} = 1$. That's true.

Go on to Choice C: $\dfrac{3}{5}$ is not equal to $\dfrac{5}{3}$ ($\dfrac{5}{3}$ is larger than $\dfrac{3}{5}$).

Choice C is the answer.

EXAMPLE 5

Thirty divided by which number is <u>not</u> a whole number?

(A) 6
(B) 5
(C) 4
(D) 30

Here again, start with the last choice, since you have to test the answers.
Choice D: 30 divided by <u>30</u> = 1. That's a whole number.
Go on to Choice C: 30 divided by <u>4</u> is <u>not</u> a whole number because there is a remainder. Choice C is correct.

EXAMPLE 6

Which has the same shape as the figure: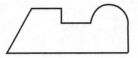

(A) 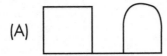   (C)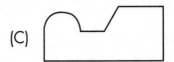

(B)    (D)

Start with Choice D because you have to try the choices.
   Choice D:

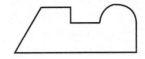

That's the same shape as the given figure. So Choice D is correct.

EXAMPLE 7

Which is equal to 6?

(A) $\dfrac{6}{6}$

(B) $\dfrac{24}{6}$

(C) $\dfrac{30}{5}$

(D) $\dfrac{5}{30}$

Since you have to test the choices, start with the last choice, D: $\dfrac{5}{30}$ is not equal to 6.

Try Choice C: $\dfrac{30}{5} = 6$. Choice C is correct.

Important Note: *On some advanced tests you'll be given five choices. So when you have to test the choices, start with Choice E.*

Now have your child try the following exercises.

QUESTIONS

1 Which is equal to 12?
- (A) 4×4
- (B) 6×6
- (C) 12×0
- (D) 1×12

2 Which figure has four equal sides?
- (A) a rectangle
- (B) a parallelogram
- (C) a square
- (D) a triangle

3 Twenty divided by which number is <u>not</u> a whole number?
- (A) 5
- (B) 10
- (C) 6
- (D) 20

4 Which is <u>not</u> true?
- (A) $\dfrac{4}{9} = \dfrac{8}{18}$
- (B) $\dfrac{3}{4} = \dfrac{6}{8}$
- (C) $\dfrac{1}{2} = \dfrac{3}{6}$
- (D) $\dfrac{3}{5} = \dfrac{6}{9}$

5 Which is true?
- (A) $680 > 697$
- (B) $680 > 680$
- (C) $680 > 796$
- (D) $680 > 524$

6 Which figure has the same shape as the following?

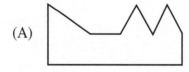
(A)

(C)

(B)

(D)

7 Which is equal to 5?
- (A) $\dfrac{5}{5}$
- (B) $\dfrac{25}{6}$
- (C) $\dfrac{4}{20}$
- (D) $\dfrac{20}{4}$

SOLUTIONS

1 (D) Since you have to test to see which choice is right, start with the last choice, Choice D: $1 \times 12 = 12$. That's the answer—no need to look at the other choices.

2 (C) You have to test the choices. Start with the last choice, Choice D: A <u>triangle</u> does not have four equal sides. In fact it has only <u>three</u> sides. Rule Choice D out.

Next look at Choice C: A <u>square</u> has four equal sides. That's the answer. No need to look at the other choices.

3 (C) You're testing out choices, so start with the last choice, Choice D: 20 divided by <u>20</u> is a whole number (1). So that's not the right answer.

Now try Choice C: 20 divided by <u>6</u> is <u>not</u> a whole number. There's a remainder when you divide. So Choice C is correct. No need to look at any of the other choices.

4 (D) You have to try the choices, so start with the last choice, Choice D.

$$\frac{3}{5} = \frac{6}{9}$$

Method 1.

Remember the shortcut for comparing which fraction is larger?

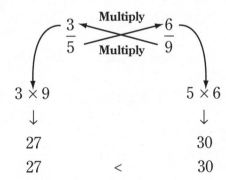

So $\dfrac{3}{5}$ is <u>less than</u> $\dfrac{6}{9}$, which means they're <u>not equal.</u> Choice D is correct.

Method 2.

Remember, you can multiply numerator and denominator by the same number and not change the value of the fraction. So look at Choice D:

$$\frac{3}{5} = \frac{6}{9}$$

Multiply numerator and denominator of $\dfrac{3}{5}$ by 2:

$$\frac{3}{5} \times \frac{2}{2} = \frac{6}{10}$$

You end up with $\dfrac{6}{10}$.

So $\dfrac{3}{5} = \dfrac{6}{10}$ and $\underline{not}\ \dfrac{6}{9}$. Thus $\dfrac{3}{5}$ is not equal to $\dfrac{6}{9}$ and so Choice D is correct.

You should determine which of these two methods (Method 1 or Method 2) you feel more comfortable with.

5 (D) Since you have to test out the choices, start with Choice D: 680 > 524. Since > means "greater than," it is true that 680 > 524. Choice D is correct. No need to look at the other choices.

6 (D) Since you have to look at the choices to match the figure in the choice with the given figure, look at Choice D first. You can see that the figure in Choice D is the same as the given figure. So Choice D is correct. No need to look at the other choices.

7 (D) Since you're looking for which of the choices is equal to 5, start with Choice   D: $\dfrac{20}{4} = 5$ (since $5 \times 4 = 20$).   So

Choice D is correct. No need to look at the other choices.

MATH STRATEGY 6:
Use Visual Thinking

Many questions involving figures can usually be answered just by seeing what the figure looks like.

Did you know that you can answer almost any geometry question on a standardized test without ever having taken a course in geometry? All you have to do is to *visualize* the solution.

Here are two clever rules:

Rule 1:
If the lines, angles, etc., look equal in the figure, they probably are.

Rule 2:
If the lines, angles, etc., look like they have a certain value, they probably do.

Below are some examples of problems that require visual thinking. But first look at the rules concerning various forms, which precede them.

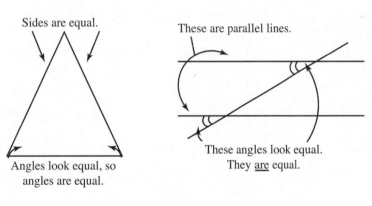

Sides are equal.

Angles look equal, so angles are equal.

These are parallel lines.

These angles look equal. They <u>are</u> equal.

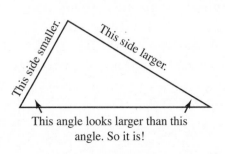

This side smaller.   This side larger.

This angle looks larger than this angle. So it is!

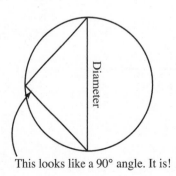

Diameter

This looks like a 90° angle. It is!

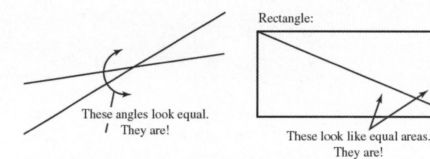

These angles look equal.
/   They are!

Rectangle:

These look like equal areas.
They are!

EXAMPLE 1

Which figure has one half of its area shaded?

(A)

(C)

(B)

(D)

Visualize! Doesn't it look like the line in the triangle (Choice C) divides the triangle in half? Well, it does! So the shaded area is one half the total area. Choice C is correct.

EXAMPLE 2

Which angles in the figure are equal?

(A) 1 and 2
(B) 2 and 3
(C) 1 and 4
(D) 1 and 3

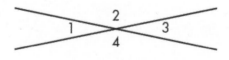

Visualize! Doesn't it look like angles 1 and 3 are equal and angles 2 and 4 are equal? They are! So Choice D is correct. Remember: You should also work from Choice D backward, since you are testing choices (Strategy 5).

Have your child try these exercises:

EXERCISES

1 If the area of the whole rectangle is 50 square meters, what is the area of the shaded portion of the rectangle?

(A) 50 (B) 35 (C) 25 (D) 10

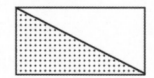

2 If two sides of the triangle are equal, which angles are equal?

(A) 1 and 2 (B) 2 and 3 (C) 1 and 3 (D) cannot tell

SOLUTIONS

1 (C) Visualize! The shaded portion of the rectangle looks like it is one half the whole rectangle. It is! So 1/2 of 50 = 25. Choice C is correct.

2 (B) Visualize! It looks like angles 2 and 3 are equal. They are! Choice B is correct.

QUANTITATIVE COMPARISON

The quantitative comparison question has been used more and more on standardized tests. In this type of question, the student is asked to compare quantities in two columns. He or she is asked to find whether the quantity in the first column is greater, less than, or equal to the quantity in the second column.

Here's a very simple example just to illustrate this type of question:

EXAMPLE

Column A	**Column B**
2	1

Choose A if the quantity under Column A is <u>greater than</u> the number under Column B.

Choose B if the quantity under Column A is <u>less than</u> the number under Column B.

Choose C if the quantity under Column A is <u>equal to</u> the number under Column B.

SOLUTION

Since 2 is greater than 1, you would choose A as the correct answer.

There are many questions of the quantitative comparison type much more difficult than the example above that will take a student a long time to answer and subject the student to mistakes if he or she doesn't know certain strategies.

Here are two rules that you and your child will discover for yourselves as you become more familiar with the strategies, but it's a good idea to see them now and be aware of them:

1 You can always *add* or *subtract* the *same quantity* to both columns and still get the *same comparison* between the columns.

2 You can always *multiply* or *divide both* columns by the *same positive number* and still get the *same comparison* between the columns.

QUANTITATIVE COMPARISON STRATEGY 1:
Cancel Numbers Common to Both Columns

EXAMPLE 1

Column A	Column B
35 + 49	49 + 36

Remember:

Choose A if Column A is greater than Column B.
Choose B if Column B is greater than Column A.
Choose C if the columns are equal.

How do you think this problem should be approached? Should we add the 35 + 49 under Column A and then compare the sum with that of 49 + 36 under Column B? That's probably the way you were taught to do such problems, but it's not the easiest or most direct way. Since in quantitative comparison questions you are not asked to find actual results or answers, but only to *compare* the columns, it isn't necessary to calculate what's under each column. After all, if the test maker had wanted your child just to do a straight calculation, he or she would have used the question in the regular multiple-choice math section, not in the quantitative comparison section.

Here's the strategy: *Get rid of quantities common to both columns.*
In the example above, get rid of the 49 that appears in both columns:

Column A	Column B
35 + ~~49~~	~~49~~ + 36
↓	↓
This leaves 35	36

Since 35 is less than 36, Column A is less than Column B. Choice B is therefore correct.

This strategy also works if numbers are subtracted. For example:

EXAMPLE 2

Column A	Column B
49 – 35	50 – 35

The way to solve this is to cancel the 35 from both columns:

Column A	Column B
49 – ~~35~~	50 – ~~35~~
↓	↓
49	50

Column B is greater than Column A, so Choice B is correct.

   Your child will save a lot of time once he or she masters this canceling strategy.

Let's look at an example that deals with multiplication:

EXAMPLE 3

Column A	Column B
$9 \times 3 \times 7$	$9 \times 7 \times 2$

Whatever you do, don't multiply the numbers in each column. Cancel the common 9 and 7 from both columns.

Column A	Column B
$\cancel{9} \times 3 \times \cancel{7}$	$\cancel{9} \times \cancel{7} \times 2$
↓	↓
3	2

Column A is greater than Column B, so Choice A is correct.

Now let's look at an example that deals with division:

EXAMPLE 4

Column A	Column B
$\dfrac{14 - 5}{7}$	$\dfrac{15 - 7}{7}$

Immediately cancel the 7's in the denominator!

Column A	Column B
$\dfrac{14-5}{\cancel{7}}$	$\dfrac{15-7}{\cancel{7}}$
↓	↓
$14 - 5$	$15 - 7$
↓	↓
9	8

Column A is greater than Column B, so Choice A is correct.

After you have shown your child the previous strategy, have him or her try the following exercises.

Remember:

Choose A if Column A is greater than Column B.
Choose B if Column A is less than Column B.
Choose C if the columns are equal.

EXERCISES

	Column A	Column B
1	$31+81$	$81+32$
2	$81-32$	$82-32$
3	$4\times7\times3$	$3\times6\times4$
4	$13\times4\times2$	$13\times4\times1$
5	136×137	136×138
6	$\dfrac{15}{7}$	$\dfrac{14}{7}$
7	$\dfrac{20-9}{5}$	$\dfrac{21-10}{5}$
8*	$1-.01$	$1+.01$
9*	$31-72$	$31-74$

*Give this to your child only if he or she is used to working with negative numbers.

SOLUTIONS

1 (B) Cancel 81 from both columns.

2 (B) Cancel 32 (or −32) from both columns.

3 (A) Cancel the 4 and the 3 from both columns to get 7 in Column A and 6 in Column B.

4 (A) Cancel the 13 and 4 from both columns to get 2 in Column A and 1 in Column B.

5 (B) Cancel the 136 from both columns to get 137 in Column A and 136 in Column B.

6 (A) Cancel the 7 in the denominator of both columns to get 15 in Column A and 14 in Column B.

7 (C) Cancel the 5 in the denominator in both columns to get $20 - 9$ in Column A and $21 - 10$ in Column B. Since $20 - 9 = 11$ and $21 - 10 = 11$, the columns are equal.

8* (B) Cancel the 1 from both columns to get $-.01$ for Column A and $+.01$ for Column B. Since $-.01$ is less than $+.01$, Column A is less than Column B.

9* (A) Cancel the 31 from both columns to get -72 in Column A and -74 in Column B. Since 72 is less than 74, -72 is greater than -74.

QUANTITATIVE COMPARISON STRATEGY 2: To Simplify, You Can Multiply, Divide, Add, or Subtract the Same Number in Both Columns

Remember:

Choose A if Column A is greater than Column B.
Choose B if Column A is less than Column B.
Choose C if the columns are equal.

EXAMPLE 1

Column A	Column B
$190 - 19$	180

Instead of subtracting $190 - 19$, *add* 19 to both columns:

Column A	Column B
$190 - \cancel{19} + \cancel{19}$	$180 + 19$
$\downarrow$	$\downarrow$
190	199

Column A is less than Column B, so Choice B is correct.
   We *added* 19 to both columns to *get rid of the minus sign* in Column A, since it's easier to add than subtract in this case.
   Here's a problem where you'd *subtract* instead of *add*.

EXAMPLE 2

Column A	Column B
424 + 478	479 + 423

Don't add yet!

You can see that the 478 in Column A is just 1 less than the 479 in Column B. You can also see that the 424 in Column A is just 1 more than the 423 in Column B. Let's subtract 423 from both columns.

Column A	Column B

Subtract 423 from both columns

Column A	Column B
424 + 478	479 + 423
↓	↓
424 + 478 − 423	479 + 423 − 423
↓	↓
478 + 424 − 423	479 + ~~423~~ − ~~423~~
↓	↓
478 + 1	479
↓	↓
479	479

Column A equals Column B, so Choice C is correct.

Here's an example that requires *multiplying* each column by the same number. (This type of problem is explained in the "Math Shortcuts" section on page 125.)

EXAMPLE 3

Column A	Column B
$\dfrac{4}{7}$	$\dfrac{5}{9}$

Use the following strategy: Try to get rid of denominators—they make things difficult. Do this by first multiplying Column A and Column B by 7. This cancels the 7 in the Column A denominator:

Column A	Column B
$\dfrac{4}{7} \times 7 \ (=4)$	$\dfrac{5}{9} \times 7$

Now multiply both columns by 9 to get rid of the denominator in Column B:

Column A	Column B
4×9	$\dfrac{5}{\cancel{9}} \times 7 \times \cancel{9}$
$\downarrow$	$\downarrow$
36	35

Column A is greater than Column B, so Choice A is correct.

Now after you have shown your child the previous strategy, have him or her try the following exercises.

Remember:

Choose A if Column A is greater than Column B.
Choose B if Column A is less than Column B.
Choose C if the columns are equal.

	Column A	Column B
1	$189 - 95$	100
2	$101 + 99$	199
3	$171 + 45$	$145 + 71$
4	$123 - 42$	$111 - 30$
5	$\dfrac{3}{4}$	$\dfrac{7}{9}$
6	$\dfrac{2}{3}$	$\dfrac{3}{4}$
7	$\dfrac{3}{7} - \dfrac{1}{5}$	$\dfrac{7}{16} - \dfrac{1}{5}$
8	$\dfrac{3}{7} - \dfrac{1}{8}$	$\dfrac{2}{8}$
9	$\dfrac{4}{3} - \dfrac{1}{2}$	$\dfrac{3}{2}$
10	$\dfrac{15 - 7}{16}$	$\dfrac{14 - 9}{16}$

SOLUTIONS

1 (B) Add 95 to both columns:

Column A	**Column B**
$189 - \cancel{95} + \cancel{95}$	$100 + 95$
$\downarrow$	$\downarrow$
189	195

Column A is less than Column B.

2 (A) Subtract 99 from both columns:

Column A	**Column B**
$101 + \cancel{99} - \cancel{99}$	$199 - 99$
$\downarrow$	$\downarrow$
101	100

Column A is greater than Column B.

3 (C) Subtract 45 from both columns:

Column A	**Column B**
$171 + \cancel{45}$	$145 + 71$
$- \cancel{45}$	$- 45$
$\downarrow$	$\downarrow$
171	$100 + 71$
$\downarrow$	$\downarrow$
171	171

Column A equals Column B.

4 (C)   **Column A**   **Column B**

Add 42 to both columns:

Column A	**Column B**
$123 - \cancel{42}$	$111 - 30$
$+ \cancel{42}$	$+ 42$
$\downarrow$	$\downarrow$
123	$153 - 30$

Add 30 to both columns:

Column A	**Column B**
$123 + 30$	$153 - \cancel{30} + \cancel{30}$
$\downarrow$	$\downarrow$
153	153

Column A equals Column B.

5 (B) <u>**Column A**</u>   <u>**Column B**</u>

$$\frac{3}{4}$$ $$\frac{7}{9}$$

Multiply both columns by 4:

$$\frac{3}{\cancel{4}} \times \cancel{4}$$ $$\frac{7}{9} \times 4$$

$$\downarrow$$ $$\downarrow$$

$$3$$ $$\frac{28}{9}$$

Multiply both columns by 9:

$$3 \times 9$$ $$\frac{28}{\cancel{9}} \times \cancel{9}$$

$$\downarrow$$ $$\downarrow$$

$$27$$ $$28$$

Column A is less than Column B.

6 (B)   <u>**Column A**</u>   <u>**Column B**</u>

$$\frac{2}{3}$$ $$\frac{3}{4}$$

Multiply both columns by 3:

$$\frac{2}{\cancel{3}} \times \cancel{3}$$ $$\frac{3}{4} \times 3$$

$$\downarrow$$ $$\downarrow$$

$$2$$ $$\frac{9}{4}$$

Multiply both columns by 4:

$$2 \times 4$$ $$\frac{9}{\cancel{4}} \times \cancel{4}$$

$$\downarrow$$ $$\downarrow$$

$$8$$ $$9$$

Column A is less than Column B.

7 (B) This solution is tricky!

<u>**Column A**</u>   <u>**Column B**</u>

$$\frac{3}{7} - \frac{1}{5}$$ $$\frac{7}{16} - \frac{1}{5}$$

First cancel common $\dfrac{1}{5}$:

$$\dfrac{3}{7} - \dfrac{1}{\cancel{5}} \qquad\qquad \dfrac{7}{16} - \dfrac{1}{\cancel{5}}$$

Next multiply by 7:

$$\dfrac{3}{7} \times \cancel{7} \qquad\qquad \dfrac{7}{16} \times 7$$

$$\downarrow \qquad\qquad\quad \downarrow$$

$$3 \qquad\qquad\quad \dfrac{49}{16}$$

Now multiply both columns by 16:

$$3 \times 16 \qquad\qquad \dfrac{49}{\cancel{16}} \times \cancel{16}$$

$$\downarrow \qquad\qquad\qquad \downarrow$$

$$48 \qquad\qquad\qquad 49$$

Column A is less than Column B.

8 (A) Add $\dfrac{1}{8}$ to both columns:

Column A	**Column B**
$\dfrac{3}{7} - \dfrac{1}{8}$	$\dfrac{2}{8}$
$\dfrac{3}{7} - \dfrac{1}{\cancel{8}} + \dfrac{1}{\cancel{8}}$	$\dfrac{2}{8} + \dfrac{1}{8}$
$\downarrow$	$\downarrow$
$\dfrac{3}{7}$	$\dfrac{3}{8}$

Since $7 < 8$, $\dfrac{3}{7} > \dfrac{3}{8}$ (Column A is greater than Column B.)

9 (B) Add $\dfrac{1}{2}$ to both columns:

Column A	**Column B**
$\dfrac{4}{3} - \dfrac{1}{2}$	$\dfrac{3}{2}$
$\dfrac{4}{3} - \dfrac{\cancel{1}}{\cancel{2}} + \dfrac{\cancel{1}}{\cancel{2}}$	$\dfrac{3}{2} + \dfrac{1}{2}$
$\downarrow$	$\downarrow$
$\dfrac{4}{3}$	$\dfrac{4}{2}$

Since 3 > 2, and the numerators are the same, $\dfrac{4}{3} < \dfrac{4}{2}$ (Column A is less than Column B.)

10 (A) Multiply both columns by 16:

Column A	**Column B**
$\dfrac{15-7}{16}$	$\dfrac{14-9}{16}$
$\dfrac{15-7}{\cancel{16}} \times \cancel{16}$	$\dfrac{14-9}{\cancel{16}} \times \cancel{16}$
$\downarrow$	$\downarrow$
$15-7$	$14-9$
$\downarrow$	$\downarrow$
8	5

Column A is greater than Column B.

QUANTITATIVE COMPARISON STRATEGY 3: Use Common Sense to Answer Questions

Often common sense can be used to answer quantitative comparison questions. Your child should use common sense whenever possible instead of racking his or her brains to solve certain problems. The less "brain-racking" there is on the test, the less exhausted your child will become and the more confident he or she will be when attacking the remaining questions.

Here are some examples of especially when to use common sense:

Remember:

Choose A if Column A is greater than Column B.
Choose B if Column A is less than Column B.
Choose C if Column A is equal to Column B.

EXAMPLE 1

Column A
Length of time
needed to travel
60 kilometers
at 30 kilometers per hour

Column B
Length of time needed
to travel 40 kilometers
at 30 kilometers per hour

It is obvious that it would take longer to travel 60 kilometers than it would to travel 40 kilometers, if the rate of travel (30 kph) is the same. There is no need to memorize any formulas about rate and time. Choice A is correct.

EXAMPLE 2

Column A
Distance around circle

Column B
Distance around triangle

Since the shortest distance between any two points is a straight line, each of the sides of the triangle has a shorter distance than the arc of the circle it cuts. So the sum of all the arcs (the whole circle) must be larger than the sum of the sides of the triangle (the distance around the triangle). Choice A is correct.

EXAMPLE 3

Column A
Number of days
in 7 months and
6 weeks

Column B
Number of days
in 6 months and
7 weeks

It should be clear that since a month is almost four times longer than a week, 7 months and 6 weeks is longer than 6 months and 7 weeks. There is no need to calculate the exact amount of days. Choice A is correct.

Now after you have shown your child the previous strategy, have him or her try the following exercises.

Remember:

Choose A if Column A is greater than Column B.
Choose B if Column A is less than Column B.
Choose C if the columns are equal.

EXERCISES

Column A	Column B
1 Number of minutes in 3 minutes and 2 hours	Number of minutes in 3 hours and 2 minutes

2 Area of circle   Area of square

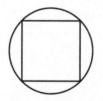

Column A	Column B
3 Length from A to B	Length from A to B and back to A

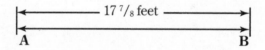

SOLUTIONS

1 (B) An hour is 60 minutes, so you should see that 3 hours and 2 minutes has many more minutes than 2 hours and 3 minutes. Column A is less than Column B.

2 (A) You can see that the square is inside the circle and thus smaller than the circle in area. Column A is greater than Column B.

3 (B) Don't add $17\frac{7}{8} + 17\frac{7}{8}$! It is obvious that traveling *back and forth* is greater (in length) than traveling one way. Choice B is correct. Thus Column A is less than Column B.

MATH REFRESHER/REVIEW
(Essential Math Skills)

Math Words, Concepts, and Rules Your Child Should Know

The following are some basic math terms and principles that your child will need to know in order to understand many of the questions on math tests.

WORDS

TRIANGLE. Any three-sided figure.

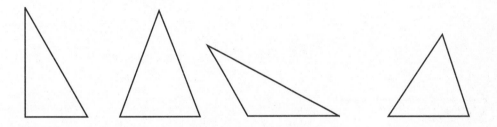

RECTANGLE. Four-sided figure with opposite sides equal and parallel. Sides must meet at right angles.

SQUARE. Four sided figure with all four sides equal; opposite sides parallel. Sides meet at right angles.

PARALLELOGRAM. Four-sided figure with opposite sides equal and parallel. Sides do not have to meet at right angles (as in a rectangle).

CIRCLE. A closed curve whose distance from a central point to any point on the curve is always the same. This distance is called the *radius* (r). The distance around the curve itself is known as the *circumference.* The *diameter* is twice the radius.

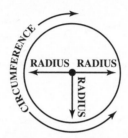

PERIMETER. Perimeter means the *length around* a figure.

EXAMPLES

Perimeter of triangle = sum of sides = 3 + 4 + 5 = 12

Perimeter of rectangle = sum of sides = 3 + 7 + 3 + 7 = 20

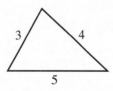

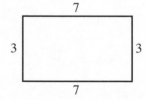

Perimeter of square = sum of sides = 3 + 3 + 3 + 3 = 12 (or 3 × 4 = 12)

Perimeter of parallelogram = sum of sides = 3 + 4 + 3 + 4 = 14

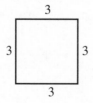

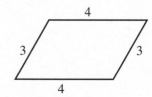

AREA OF RECTANGLE. The area of a rectangle equals its length times its width.

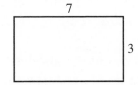

EXAMPLE

Area = length × width = 7 × 3 = 21

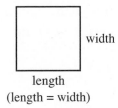

AREA OF SQUARE. The area of a square equals its length times its width.

EXAMPLE

Area = length × width = 3 × 3 = 9

GREATER THAN, LESS THAN, AND EQUAL TO SYMBOLS

Greater than can be written as >.
Less than can be written as <.
Equal to can be written as = .

EXAMPLES

300 > 299 (300 is *greater than* 299)
299 < 300 (299 is *less than* 300)
300 = 300 (300 is *equal to* 300)

Notice that 300 > 299 can also be written as 299 < 300 (299 is *less than* 300) and 299 < 300 can also be written as 300 > 299 (300 is *greater than* 299).

From two unequal relations, you can sometimes find a third relation.
Example: Mary > Sam, and Sam > John.
    Then Mary > John.

What this really says is that if the *first is greater than the second* and the *second is greater than the third*, then the *first is greater than the third*.

FRACTIONS

A fraction has a *numerator* and a *denominator.* The numerator is the number on top, and the denominator the one on the bottom. The numerator is *divided* by the denominator.

EXAMPLE

$\frac{3}{7}$ numerator ← division sign ← denominator

When fractions have the *same numerator* but *different denominators,* the one with the *larger denominator is smaller.*

EXAMPLE

$\frac{1}{8} < \frac{1}{4}$

When fractions have the *same denominator* but *different numerators,* the fraction with the *larger numerator* is *larger.*

EXAMPLE

$$\frac{3}{7} > \frac{2}{7}$$

You can *multiply both numerator and denominator* by the *same number* and *not change the value of the fraction.*

EXAMPLE

$$\frac{3}{4}$$

$$\frac{3}{4} \times \frac{3}{3} = \frac{9}{12}; \frac{9}{12} = \frac{3}{4}$$

EQUALS *(Rules for Adding, Subtracting, Multiplying and Dividing)*

1 *Equals added to equals are equal.*

EXAMPLE

$$\begin{array}{r} 3 = 3 \\ + \ 4 = 4 \\ \hline 7 = 7 \end{array}$$

2 *Equals subtracted from equals are equal*

EXAMPLE

$$\begin{array}{r} 4 = 4 \\ - \ 3 = 3 \\ \hline 1 = 1 \end{array}$$

3 *You can multiply equals by equals to get equals.*

EXAMPLE

$$\begin{array}{r} 3 = 3 \\ \times \ 2 = 2 \\ \hline 6 = 6 \end{array}$$

4 *You can divide equals by equals to get equals.*

EXAMPLE

$$\begin{array}{r} 6 = 6 \\ \div \ 2 = 2 \\ \hline 3 = 3 \end{array}$$

EVEN AND ODD INTEGERS (Rules for Adding, Subtracting, Multiplying, and Dividing)

An *even integer* is a whole number *exactly divisible by 2* (2, 4, 6, 8, 10, 12, etc.). An *odd integer* is a whole number *not exactly divisible by 2* (1, 3, 5, 7, 9, 11, etc.).

1 An *even integer* plus or minus another even integer always equals an *even integer*.
For example: $4 + 6 = 10$; $6 - 4 = 2$.

2 An *even integer* plus or minus an *odd integer* always equals an *odd integer*.
For example: $4 + 1 = 5$; $4 - 3 = 1$.

3 An *odd integer* plus or minus another *odd integer* always equals an *even integer*.
For example: $3 + 5 = 8$; $9 - 5 = 4$.

4 An *even integer* multiplied by an *even integer* always equals an *even integer*.
For example: $2 \times 4 = 8$; $4 \times 4 = 16$.

5 An *even integer* multiplied by an *odd integer* always equals an *even integer*.
For example: $2 \times 3 = 6$.

6 An *odd integer* multiplied by an *odd integer* always equals an *odd integer*.
For example: $3 \times 3 = 9$; $5 \times 7 = 35$.

7 An *even integer* divided by an *even integer* is *sometimes even, sometimes odd,* and *sometimes not an integer*.
For example: $4 \div 2 = 2$; $12 \div 4 = 3$; $10 \div 4 = 2\frac{1}{2}$; $4 \div 8 = 1/2$.

8 An *even integer* divided by an *odd integer* is *sometimes even, never odd,* or *not an integer*.
For example; $2 \div 1 = 2$; $2 \div 3 = 2/3$; $12 \div 3 = 4$; $12 \div 11 = 12/11$.

9 An *odd integer* divided by an *odd integer* is *never even, sometimes odd,* or *not an integer*.
For example: $9 \div 3 = 3$; $11 \div 9 = 11/9$.

10 An *odd integer* divided by an *even integer* is *never an integer*.
For example: $3 \div 2 = 3/2$; $5 \div 4 = 5/4$.

AVERAGES

Average means the *total number of one group of items* divided by *the number of another group of items.*

EXAMPLE 1

There are 200 students in a school with 10 classes. What is the *average number* of students in each class?

SOLUTION

$$\text{Average} = \frac{\text{Total number of students}}{\text{Number of classes}}$$

Total number of students = 200
Number of classes = 10

So average = $\dfrac{200 \text{ students}}{10 \text{ classes}}$ = 20 students per class

EXAMPLE 2

What is the average number of melons for each crate if there are 100 melons in 10 crates?

SOLUTION

Total number of melons = 100
Number of crates = 10

So average = $\dfrac{100}{10}$ = 10

PARTS

$\dfrac{1}{4}$ means 1 in 4 or 1 part in 4 parts.

EXAMPLE

What part of the rectangle is shaded?

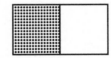

SOLUTION

1/2. Since there are *two* parts (shaded and unshaded) and *one* part is shaded, so 1/2 is shaded.

After you have explained to your child the words, concepts, and rules just described, have him or her try the following exercises.

EXERCISES

1 The perimeter of the triangle below is
   (A) 480
   (B) 48
   (C) 24
   (D) 12

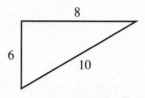

2 Which figure does *not* always have two opposite sides equal?
   (A) a parallelogram
   (B) a triangle
   (C) a rectangle
   (D) a square

3 What is the *perimeter* of the square below?
   (A) 3
   (B) 12
   (C) 9
   (D) cannot tell

4 What is the *area* of the rectangle below?
   (A) 7
   (B) 14
   (C) 12
   (D) 10

5 Which is true?
   (A) 23 > 32
   (B) 32 > 31
   (C) 33 > 35
   (D) 30 > 30

6 Which is true?
   (A) 30 < 50
   (B) 31 < 21
   (C) 21 < 21
   (D) 15 < 14

7 If $4 = 3 + \square$, then which is true?
  (A) $4 - 3 = \square$
  (B) $4 + 3 = \square$
  (C) $4 \times 3 = \square$
  (D) $4 \div 3 = \square$

8 If $3 = \square$, then which is true?
  (A) $3 \times 2 = 2 \times \square$
  (B) $3 \times 2 = 2 + \square$
  (C) $3 \times 2 = 2 - \square$
  (D) $3 \times 2 = 3 - \square$

9 Which is an even integer?
  (A) 3
  (B) 7
  (C) 9
  (D) 12

10 Which is an odd integer?
  (A) 2
  (B) 4
  (C) 8
  (D) 9

11 Which is true?
  (A) $\dfrac{2}{3} > \dfrac{2}{1}$
  (B) $\dfrac{3}{4} > \dfrac{3}{2}$
  (C) $\dfrac{4}{7} > \dfrac{4}{8}$
  (D) $\dfrac{5}{8} > \dfrac{6}{8}$

12 Which is true?
  (A) $\dfrac{2}{3} = \dfrac{6}{8}$
  (B) $\dfrac{3}{4} = \dfrac{9}{10}$
  (C) $\dfrac{3}{5} = \dfrac{6}{12}$
  (D) $\dfrac{4}{7} = \dfrac{8}{14}$

13 What is the average number of crayons per box if there are 30 boxes of crayons and a total of 900 crayons in all the boxes?
  (A) 30
  (B) 3
  (C) 90
  (D) 9

14 Which circle has 1/4 of its area shaded?
  (A)
  (C)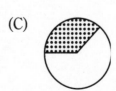
  (B)
  (D)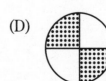

SOLUTIONS

1 (C) Perimeter equals length around.
length around = 6 + 8 + 10 = 24

2 (B) Choices:
(A) A parallelogram always has opposite sides equal.

(B) A triangle does not always have opposite sides equal.

(C) A rectangle always has opposite sides equal.

(D) A square always has opposite sides equal.

3 (B) Perimeter equals length around.
All sides of a square are equal.
So 3 + 3 + 3 + 3 = 12 or 3 × 4 = 12

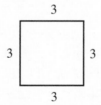

4 (C) Area of rectangle equals length times width.
length = 4, width = 3
So 4 × 3 = 12

5 (B) The sign > means greater than; < means less than.
Choices:
(A) 23 is not > 32; it is < 32
(B) 32 is > 31
(C) 33 is not > 35; it is < 35
(D) 30 is not > 30; it is = 30

6 (A) The sign < means less than; > means greater than.
Choices:
(A) 30 is < 50
(B) 31 is not < 21; 31 > 21
(C) 21 is not < 21; 21 = 21
(D) 15 is not < 14; 15 > 14

7 (A) Equals subtracted from equals are equal.

$$4 = 3 + \square$$
$$-3 = 3$$
$$4 - \cancel{3} = 3 + \square - \cancel{3}$$
$$4 - 3 = \square$$

8 (A) Equals multiplied by equals are equal.

$$3 = \square$$
$$\times 2 = 2$$
$$\overline{3 \times 2 = 2 \times \square}$$

9 (D) An even integer is a whole number exactly divisible by 2.
Choices:
(A) The number 3 is *not* exactly divisible by 2, so it is *odd*.
(B) The number 7 is *not* exactly divisible by 2, so it is *odd*.
(C) The number 9 is *not* exactly divisible by 2, so it is odd.
(D) The number 12 *is* exactly divisible by 2: 12 ÷ 2 = 6. So it is *even*.

10 (D) An odd integer is a whole number not divisible by 2.
Choices:
(A) The number 2 *is* divisible by 2, so it is *even*.
(B) The number 4 *is* divisible by 2, so it is *even*.
(C) The number 8 *is* divisible by 2, so it is *even*.
(D) The number 9 *is not* divisible by 2, so it is *odd*.

11 (C) Choices:

(A) Numerators are the same, denominator 3 is larger,

so $\dfrac{2}{3} < \dfrac{2}{1}$.

(B) Numerators are the same, denominator 4 is larger,

so $\dfrac{3}{4} < \dfrac{3}{2}$.

(C) Numerators are the same, denominator 7 is smaller,

so $\dfrac{4}{7} < \dfrac{4}{8}$.

(D) Denominators are the same, numerator 5 is smaller,

so $\dfrac{5}{8} > \dfrac{6}{8}$.

12 (D) Multiply both numerator and denominator of Choices A and B by 3, and of Choice C and D by 2. See "Fractions" section on page 126.

$$\dfrac{4}{7} \times \dfrac{2}{2} = \dfrac{8}{14}$$

Choices:

(A) $\dfrac{2}{3} \times \dfrac{3}{3} = \dfrac{6}{9}$ *not* $\dfrac{6}{8}$

(B) $\dfrac{3}{4} \times \dfrac{3}{3} = \dfrac{9}{12}$ *not* $\dfrac{9}{10}$

(C) $\dfrac{3}{5} \times \dfrac{2}{2} = \dfrac{6}{10}$ *not* $\dfrac{6}{12}$

(D) $\dfrac{4}{7} \times \dfrac{2}{2} = \dfrac{8}{14}$

13 (A) Average $= \dfrac{\text{Total}}{\text{Number of items}}$

Total = 900 crayons

Number of items = 30 boxes

$$\text{Average} = \dfrac{900}{30} = \dfrac{90\cancel{0}}{3\cancel{0}} = 30$$

14 (B) The fraction $\dfrac{1}{4}$ means 1 part in 4 parts. Of the four parts

of the circle, one is shaded, so $\dfrac{1}{4}$ of the circle is said to be shaded.

Math Shortcuts Your Child Should Know

There are many shortcuts that your child can use when working out math problems. The most important of these are discussed below.

COMPARING TWO FRACTIONS

Sometimes your child will have to find out which of two fractions is larger. Here's a typical example:

EXAMPLE 1

Which is greater:

$$\frac{3}{7} \text{ or } \frac{7}{16}?$$

You or your child may have been taught to find a common denominator first, and then compare the fractions. There's a much easier way that you should be aware of:

SOLUTION

$$16 \times 3 \qquad 7 \times 7$$
$$\downarrow \qquad\qquad \downarrow$$
$$48 \qquad\qquad 49$$

Since 48 is less than 49, $\frac{3}{7}$ (above 48) is less than $\frac{7}{16}$ (above 49).

Any two fractions can be compared in this way. Try it yourself:

EXAMPLE 2

Which is greater:

$$\frac{4}{9} \text{ or } \frac{9}{20}?$$

SOLUTION

$$80 \qquad\qquad 81$$

Since 80 is less than 81, $\frac{4}{9}$ is less than $\frac{9}{20}$.

ADDING FRACTIONS

EXAMPLE 1

What is $\dfrac{3}{5} + \dfrac{5}{7}$?

SOLUTION

Here's the quick way to add fractions:

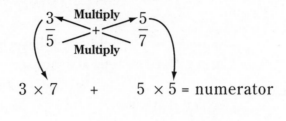

$$3 \times 7 \quad + \quad 5 \times 5 = \text{numerator}$$

$$\dfrac{3}{5} \quad + \quad \dfrac{5}{7}$$

$$5 \times 7 = 35 = \text{denominator}$$

$$\text{Result} = \frac{\text{numerator}}{\text{denominator}} = \frac{(3 \times 7) + (5 \times 5)}{35} = \frac{46}{35} = 1\frac{11}{35}$$

SUBTRACTING FRACTIONS

EXAMPLE 1

Find: $\dfrac{5}{7} - \dfrac{3}{5}$

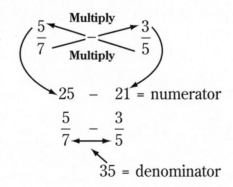

$$25 \quad - \quad 21 = \text{numerator}$$

$$\dfrac{5}{7} \quad - \quad \dfrac{3}{5}$$

$$35 = \text{denominator}$$

$$\text{Result} = \frac{\text{numerator}}{\text{denominator}} = \frac{4}{35}$$

EXAMPLE 2

What is $2 - \dfrac{1}{9}$?

Write 2 as $\dfrac{2}{1}$.

$$\dfrac{2}{1} - \dfrac{1}{9} = \left(\dfrac{2}{1} \times \dfrac{1}{9} \right)$$

$$18 - 1 = 17 = \text{numerator}$$

$$1 \times 9 = \text{denominator}$$

So, the result is $\dfrac{17}{9}$, or $1\dfrac{8}{9}$

MULTIPLYING FRACTIONS

When multiplying fractions, always try to reduce first.

EXAMPLE

Find: $\dfrac{1}{4} \times \dfrac{8}{33}$

Don't multiply 4×33!

$$\dfrac{1}{\cancel{4}} \times \dfrac{\cancel{8}^{\,2}}{33} = \dfrac{2}{33}$$

CALCULATING PERCENTS— MULTIPLY RATHER THAN DIVIDE

EXAMPLE

What percent is $\dfrac{4}{25}$?

A percent is a number divided by 100. For example, 20% or 20 percent is $\dfrac{20}{100}$. So we want to find what number divided by 100 is equal to $\dfrac{4}{25}$.

You might be tempted to divide 25 into 4. But it is usually easier to multiply than to divide. So do this:

$$\frac{4}{25} \times \frac{4}{4} = \frac{16}{100} = 16\% \text{ or } 16 \text{ percent}$$

Isn't that easier than dividing 25 into 4?

SUBTRACTING LARGE NUMBERS

EXAMPLE 1

What is 112 – 98?

You can do this mentally (not on paper) by saying to yourself:

112 – 100 = 12

100 – 98 = 2

Now just add 12 and 2 to get 14, which is the answer.

The reason this works is because 112 – 100 + 100 – 98 = 112 – 98.

EXAMPLE 2

What is 72 – 39?

Solution:

72 – 42 = 30

42 – 39 = 3

30 + 3 = 33 (answer)

Other Method:

72 – 40 = 32

40 – 39 = 1

32 + 1 = 33

Get the gist?

MULTIPLYING FRACTIONS

EXAMPLE 1

What is $3\frac{1}{2} \times 3\frac{2}{3}$?

Whenever you see something like this example, always write the two numbers as fractions. That is, write $3\frac{1}{2}$ as a fraction and write $3\frac{2}{3}$ as another fraction, then multiply.

Here's how to change $3\frac{1}{2}$ to a fraction:

To find the *numerator* for $3\frac{1}{2}$:

$$3\frac{1}{2} \quad 2 \times 3 + 1 = \text{numerator}$$

To find the *denominator* for $3\frac{1}{2}$:

$$3\frac{1}{2} \to 2 = \text{denominator}$$

$$3\frac{1}{2} = \frac{2 \times 3 + 1}{2} = \frac{6 + 1}{2} = \frac{7}{2} = \frac{\text{numerator}}{\text{denominator}}$$

To convert $3\frac{2}{3}$ as a fraction, we follow the same method we used for $3\frac{1}{2}$:

Numerator:

Then add

$$3\frac{2}{3} \quad 3 \times 3 + 2 = 11 = \text{numerator}$$

Multiply

Denominator:

$$3\frac{2}{3} \to 3 = \text{denominator}$$

$$\frac{3 \times 3 + 2}{3} = \frac{9 + 2}{3} = \frac{11}{3} = \frac{\text{numerator}}{\text{denominator}}$$

Now multiply:

$$3\frac{1}{2} \times 3\frac{2}{3} = \frac{7}{2} \times \frac{11}{3} \times \frac{77}{6} = 12\frac{5}{6} \text{ (answer)}$$

EXAMPLE 2

What is $3\dfrac{1}{2} \times 6$?

$$3\dfrac{1}{2} = \dfrac{6+1}{2} = \dfrac{7}{2}$$

$$6 = \dfrac{6}{1}$$

So:

$$3\dfrac{1}{2} \times 6 = \dfrac{7}{2} \times \dfrac{6}{1} = \dfrac{7}{\cancel{2}} \times \dfrac{\cancel{6}^{3}}{1} = 21 \text{ (answer)}$$

After you have shown your child the math shortcuts just presented, have him or her try the following exercises.

QUESTIONS

Questions 1–3. Which is greater?

1 $\dfrac{3}{7}$ or $\dfrac{6}{15}$

2 $\dfrac{3}{4}$ or $\dfrac{4}{5}$

3 $\dfrac{2}{3}$ or $\dfrac{7}{9}$

Questions 4–5. Add:

4 $\dfrac{3}{7} + \dfrac{4}{3}$

5 $\dfrac{2}{3} + \dfrac{3}{4}$

Questions 6–8. Subtract:

6 $\dfrac{2}{3} - \dfrac{1}{4}$

7 $\dfrac{3}{4} - \dfrac{2}{3}$

8 $2 - \dfrac{2}{5}$

Questions 9–10. Multiply:

9 $\dfrac{7}{8} \times \dfrac{8}{25}$

10 $\dfrac{2}{5} \times \dfrac{25}{16}$

Questions 11–14. Find what percent these fractions are:

11 $\dfrac{14}{25}$

12 $\dfrac{3}{250}$

13 $\dfrac{1}{50}$

14 $\dfrac{4}{5}$

Questions 15–17. Subtract:

Questions 18–20. Multiply:

15 $115 - 99$

18 $1\dfrac{1}{2} \times 1\dfrac{1}{2}$

16 $63 - 49$

19 $2\dfrac{1}{3} \times 2\dfrac{2}{3}$

17 $202 - 99$

20 $4\dfrac{1}{4} \times 5$

SOLUTIONS

1

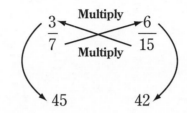

45 is greater than 42, so $\dfrac{3}{7}$ is greater than $\dfrac{6}{15}$.

2

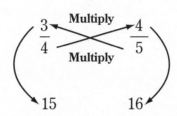

$\dfrac{3}{4}$ is less than $\dfrac{4}{5}$ since 15 is less than 16.

3

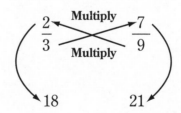

$\dfrac{2}{3}$ is less than $\dfrac{7}{9}$ since 18 is less than 21.

4

$$\frac{3}{7} + \frac{4}{3} = \frac{(3 \times 3) + (7 \times 4)}{21}$$

$$= \frac{9 + 28}{21}$$

$$= \frac{37}{21} = 1\frac{16}{21}$$

5 $\dfrac{2}{3} + \dfrac{3}{4} = \dfrac{(4 \times 2)+(3 \times 3)}{12}$

$= \dfrac{8+9}{12}$

$= \dfrac{17}{12} = 1\dfrac{5}{12}$

6 $\dfrac{2}{3} - \dfrac{1}{4} = \dfrac{(4 \times 2)-(3 \times 1)}{12}$

$= \dfrac{8 - 3}{12}$

$= \dfrac{5}{12}$

7 $\dfrac{3}{4} - \dfrac{2}{3} = \dfrac{(3 \times 3)-(4 \times 2)}{12}$

$= \dfrac{9 - 8}{12}$

$= \dfrac{1}{12}$

8 $2 - \dfrac{2}{5} = \dfrac{2}{1} - \dfrac{2}{5}$

$= \dfrac{10 - 2}{5}$

$= \dfrac{8}{5} = 1\dfrac{3}{5}$

9 $\dfrac{7}{8} \times \dfrac{8}{25} =$

$\dfrac{7}{\overset{}{\underset{1}{\cancel{8}}}} \times \dfrac{\overset{1}{\cancel{8}}}{25} = \dfrac{7}{25}$

10 $\dfrac{2}{5} \times \dfrac{25}{16} =$

$\dfrac{{}^{1}\cancel{2}}{\cancel{5}} \times \dfrac{\cancel{25}^{5}}{\cancel{16}_{8}} = \dfrac{5}{8}$

11 $\dfrac{14}{25} \times \dfrac{4}{4} = \dfrac{56}{100} = 56\%$

12 $\dfrac{3}{250} \times \dfrac{4}{4} = \dfrac{12}{1,000} = \dfrac{1.2}{100} = 1.2\%$

13 $\dfrac{1}{50} \times \dfrac{2}{2} = \dfrac{2}{100} = 2\%$

14 $\dfrac{4}{5} \times \dfrac{20}{20} = \dfrac{80}{100} = 80\%$

15 $115 - 100 = 15$

$100 - 99 = 1$

$15 + 1 = 16$

16 $63 - 50 = 13$

$50 - 49 = 1$

$13 + 1 = 14$

17 $202 - 100 = 102$

$100 - 99 = 1$

$102 + 1 = 103$

OR

$202 - 102 = 100$

$102 - 99 = 3$

$100 + 3 = 103$

18 $\quad 1\dfrac{1}{2} = \dfrac{2+1}{2} = \dfrac{3}{2}$

$\quad 1\dfrac{1}{2} \times 1\dfrac{1}{2} = \dfrac{3}{2} \times \dfrac{3}{2} = \dfrac{9}{4} = 2\dfrac{1}{4}$

19 $\quad 2\dfrac{1}{3} = \dfrac{6+1}{3} = \dfrac{7}{3}$

$\quad 2\dfrac{2}{3} = \dfrac{6+2}{3} = \dfrac{8}{3}$

$\quad 2\dfrac{1}{3} \times 2\dfrac{2}{3} = \dfrac{7}{3} \times \dfrac{8}{3} = \dfrac{56}{9} = 6\dfrac{2}{9}$

20 $\quad 4\dfrac{1}{4} = \dfrac{(4 \times 4)+1}{4} = \dfrac{17}{4}$

$\quad 5 = \dfrac{5}{1}$

$\quad 4\dfrac{1}{4} \times 5 = \dfrac{17}{4} \times \dfrac{5}{1} = \dfrac{85}{4} = 21\dfrac{1}{4}$

The Fifty Basic Math Problems for Grades 3• 4• 5

Here are fifty of the most basic math problems (for grades 3 to 5), which your child should know how to solve. After your child finishes these, check to see whether they were done correctly by comparing his or her approaches and answers with the approaches and answers given following these questions. However, don't expect your child to have every answer, or even to be able to do all of the problems, especially the last ones, because your child may not have learned in school some of the material applicable to those questions.

PROBLEMS

1
$$\begin{array}{r} 542 \\ +\ 313 \\ \hline \end{array}$$

2
$$\begin{array}{r} 7 \\ \times\ 4 \\ \hline \end{array}$$

3 $60 + 300 =$

4 $11 + 8 - 9 =$

5
$$\begin{array}{r} 271 \\ +\ 792 \\ \hline \end{array}$$

6
$$\begin{array}{r} 25 \\ \times\ 3 \\ \hline \end{array}$$

7
$$\begin{array}{r} 605 \\ \times\ 4 \\ \hline \end{array}$$

8
$$\begin{array}{r} 9 \text{ hours } 30 \text{ minutes} \\ -\ 4 \text{ hours } 10 \text{ minutes} \\ \hline \end{array}$$

9
$$\begin{array}{r} 1,171 \\ 2,211 \\ +\ 1,113 \\ \hline \end{array}$$

10
$$\begin{array}{r} \$92.79 \\ +\ \$86.39 \\ \hline \end{array}$$

11 $34 \div 2 =$

12
$$\begin{array}{r} .23 \\ \times\ 3 \\ \hline \end{array}$$

13 $1,175 - 100 =$

14
$$\begin{array}{r} 6,136 \\ +\ 2,914 \\ \hline \end{array}$$

15
$$\begin{array}{r} 10 \text{ minutes } 13 \text{ seconds} \\ +\ 41 \text{ minutes } 15 \text{ seconds} \\ \hline \end{array}$$

16
$$\begin{array}{r} 8,796 \\ +\ \ \ \ 45 \\ \hline \end{array}$$

17 $2\overline{)222}$

18
$$\begin{array}{r} 41.73 \\ +\ 9.09 \\ \hline \end{array}$$

19 $4 \times 172 =$

20
$$\begin{array}{r} 1,792 \\ 2,346 \\ +\ 3,421 \\ \hline \end{array}$$

21
$$\begin{array}{r} 1,796 \\ -\ 699 \\ \hline \end{array}$$

22 $6\overline{)246}$

23
$$\begin{array}{r} 904 \\ \times\ 80 \\ \hline \end{array}$$

24 $399 \div 3 =$

25 $4 + 2\dfrac{2}{5} =$

26 $9 \times 900 =$

27   723 tons
         $-$ 288 tons

28 $43.75
         $\times$ 4

29   8,000
         $-$ 625

30   902
         $-$ 807

31   12.3 + 7.8   =

32   7,000
        $\times$ 60

33 $7\overline{)5,021}$

34   6 hours 25 minutes
         + 3 hours 50 minutes
         (Reduce minutes answer to a number under 60)

35   96 hours = how many days?

36   215.00
         $-$ 117.81

37   72
         $\times$ 35

38 $\dfrac{6}{15}$

         $-$ $\dfrac{2}{15}$

39 $33\overline{)693}$

40 $\dfrac{1}{4}$ $\dfrac{1}{2}$ =

41 $\dfrac{7}{10}$ = (express as decimal)

42 $\dfrac{2}{3}$ of 9 =

43 $(24 \times 30) - (24 \times 3) =$

44 $5\overline{)15.05}$ =

45 $\dfrac{4}{9} = \dfrac{\square}{36}$ What is "$\square$" ?

46   100 cm = 1 m (meter)
         303 cm + 707 cm = how many meters?
         (express in decimal form)

47   8.4
        $\times 7.6$

48   4 hours 30 minutes
         $\times$ 3
         (reduce minutes answer to a number under 60)

49 $5\dfrac{1}{3} \times 3\dfrac{1}{8} =$

50 $3\dfrac{1}{3}$
         $-1\dfrac{2}{3}$

Solutions to the Fifty Basic Math Problems

1
$$542$$
$$+\ 313 \text{ (add units, tens, and hundreds)}$$
$$855 \qquad \boxed{855}$$

2
$$7$$
$$\times\ 4$$
$$\boxed{28} \quad \text{(know multiplication table)}$$

3 $60 + 300$

Rewrite:
$$60$$
$$+\ 300$$
$$\boxed{360} \text{ (put units under units, tens under tens)}$$

4 $11 + 8 - 9$

Add $11 + 8$ first.

You get 19.

Now subtract: $19 - 9$
$$19$$
$$-\ 9$$
$$\boxed{10}$$

5
$$\overset{1}{271} \quad \text{(carry the 1, since } 7 + 9 = 16)$$
$$+\ 792$$
$$\boxed{1063}$$

6
$$25 \qquad 5 \times 3 = 15 \quad \text{Add 1}$$
$$\times\ {}_1 3$$
$$\boxed{75} \quad 2 \times 3 = 6;\ 6 + 1 = 7 \text{ (You carry the 1 from the 15.)}$$

7
$$605 \qquad 5 \times 4 = 20 \quad \text{Add 2}$$
$$\times_2\ 4$$
$$\overline{2{,}420} \quad 4 \times 0 = 0;\ 0 + 2 = 2 \text{ (You carry the 2 from the 20.)}$$

8   9 hours 30 minutes   (subtract minutes; subtract hours)
    − 4 hours 10 minutes
      $\boxed{5 \text{ hours } 20 \text{ minutes}}$

9   1,171 (add units, tens, hundreds, thousands)
    2,211
    + 1,113
      $\boxed{4,495}$

10 $\overset{1\ 1}{\$92.79}$ (carry 1, since 9 + 9 = **18**)
    + $86.39   (carry 1, since **1** + 7 + 3 = **11**)
      $\boxed{\$179.18}$
      ↑ (put decimal right under other decimals)

11   34 ÷ 2 = 2$\overline{)34}$

    17
    2$\overline{)34}$ = $\boxed{17}$
    2↓
    14

12   .23
    ×   3
      $\boxed{.69}$
          ↖ (two decimal places to left since .23
             has decimal two places to left)

13   1,175 − 100
    Rewrite :
      1,175
    −   100
      $\boxed{1,075}$

14 $\overset{1\ 1}{6,136}$
    + 2,914   6 + 4 = **10**, carry 1
      $\boxed{9,050}$ 1 + 9 = **10**, carry 1

15   10 minutes, 13 seconds   (add seconds, add minutes)
+   41 minutes 15 seconds
$\boxed{\text{51 minutes 28 seconds}}$

16 $\overset{1\,1}{8{,}796}$ $6 + 5 = \mathbf{11}, \text{carry } 1$
+   45 $1 + 9 + 4 = \mathbf{14}, \text{carry } 1$
$\boxed{8{,}841}$

17 $\begin{array}{r}111 \\ 2\overline{)222} \\ \underline{2} \\ 02 \\ \underline{2} \\ 02 \end{array}$ $\boxed{111}$

18 $\overset{1\,\ 1}{41.73}$ $3 + 9 = \mathbf{12}, \text{carry } 1$
+   9.09 $\mathbf{1} + 9 = \mathbf{10}, \text{carry } 1$
$\boxed{50.82}$

19 4×172

Rewrite
172
$\times\ _2\ 4$ $2 \times 4 = 8 \text{ (units)}$
$\boxed{688}$ $7 \times 4 = 28 \text{ (tens)}$
$\uparrow$
carry 2 $\searrow$
$4 \times 1 = 4 + 2 = 6 \text{ (hundreds)}$

20 $\overset{1\ \ 1}{1{,}792}$ Add units : 2
2,346   6
+   3,421 $\underline{+\ 1}$
7,559   9

$\boxed{7{,}559}$ Add tens : 9
4
$\underline{+\ 2}$
15
$\nearrow$

Carry 1 to hundreds column.

Add hundreds, remembering to carry 1:

$$
\begin{array}{r}
{\scriptstyle 1} \\
7 \\
3 \\
+\ 4 \\
\hline
15
\end{array}
$$

↗

Carry 1 to thousands.

Add thousands, carrying 1:

$$
\begin{array}{r}
{\scriptstyle 1} \\
1 \\
2 \\
+\ 3 \\
\hline
7
\end{array}
$$

21

$$
\begin{array}{r}
{\scriptstyle 6\ 8} \\
1,796 \\
-\quad 699 \\
\hline
\boxed{1,097}
\end{array}
$$

6 – 9 doesn't go, so make it
16 – 9, borrowing 1 from tens in 1,796:

16 – 9 = 7

1,097

8 – 9 doesn't go, so make it
18 – 9, borrowing 1 from hundreds in 1,796:

18 – 9 = 9

6 – 6 = 0

1 – (0) = 1

22

$$
\begin{array}{r}
41 \\
6\overline{)246} \\
24\downarrow \\
\hline
06
\end{array}
$$

$\boxed{4} \times 6 = 24$

$\boxed{1} \times 6 = 6$

23

$$
\begin{array}{r}
904 \\
\times\ \ 80
\end{array}
\quad\rightarrow\quad
\begin{array}{r}
904 \\
\times\ \ 80 \\
\hline
0
\end{array}
$$

(since 80 ends in 0, move 80 to right)

$$
\begin{array}{r}
904 \\
\times\quad 80 \\
\hline
\boxed{72,320}
\end{array}
$$

24 $399 \div 3$

Rewrite:

$$
\begin{array}{r}
133 \\
3)\overline{399} \\
\underline{3}\!\downarrow \\
09 \\
\underline{9}\!\downarrow \\
09
\end{array}
\qquad \boxed{133}
$$

25 $4 + 2\dfrac{2}{5} = 6\dfrac{2}{5}$ or

Rewrite:

$$
\begin{array}{r}
4 \\
+\,2\dfrac{2}{5} \\
\hline
\boxed{6\dfrac{2}{5}}
\end{array}
$$

26 9×900

Rewrite:

$$
\begin{array}{r}
900 \\
\times\quad 9 \\
\hline
\boxed{8,100}
\end{array}
$$

27
$$
\begin{array}{r}
\overset{61}{7\!\!\!/23}\text{ tons} \\
-\quad 288\text{ tons} \\
\hline
435\text{ tons}
\end{array}
$$
$\leftarrow$ borrow 1

(Keep "tons" under "tons")

$$\boxed{435\text{ tons}}$$

28

$\swarrow$ (two decimal places)

$$
\begin{array}{r}
\$43.75 \\
\times\qquad 4 \\
\hline
\$\qquad .
\end{array}
$$

(keep \$ sign) $\nearrow$ $\nwarrow$ (two decimal places)

$$
\begin{array}{r}
\$43.75 \\
\times\qquad {}_{2}4 \\
\hline
0
\end{array}
\qquad 5 \times 4 = 20
$$
$\uparrow$
carry 2

$43.75
× ₃ ₂4   7 × 4 = 28
$ .00   28 + 2 = 30
                       ↑
                   carry 3

$43.75
× ₁ ₃ ₂4   4 × 3 = 12
$ 5.00   12 + 3 = 15
                       ↑
                   carry 1

43.75
×   4   4 × 4 = 16
$175.00   16 + 1 = 17
      ↓
  $175.00

29   ⁷ ⁹ ⁹
        8̸, 0̸0̸0̸
      −   625   (borrow 1 from 0 [10])
        7, 375   (borrow 1 from 8 in thousands)

30   ⁸⁹
         9̸0̸2   (borrow 1 from 0 [10] in tens)
       −   807   (borrow 1 from 9 in hundreds)
            95

31 12.3 + 7.8
Rewrite :

      12.3
  +   7.8
        ·
        ↑
(Keep decimal under decimals above)

    ¹ ¹
    12.3   3 + 8 = 11 carry 1
  + 7.8   1 + 2 + 7 = 10 carry 1
    20.1

32   7,000
$\underline{\times \quad 60}$

(move 60 right, since it ends in 0)

7,000
$\underline{\times \quad 60}$
$\boxed{420,000}$

33
$$7)\overline{5,021} \quad \begin{array}{c}717\end{array}$$

$\begin{array}{r} 717 \\ 7)\overline{5,021} \\ \underline{4\ 9}\downarrow \\ 12 \\ \underline{\ 7} \\ 51 \\ \underline{49} \\ 2 \end{array}$

$\boxed{\begin{array}{l} 717 \text{ remainder } 2 \\ \text{or } 717\dfrac{2}{7} \end{array}}$

34   6 hours 25 minute   (add minutes, add hours)
$\underline{+\ 3 \text{ hours } 50 \text{ minutes}}$
9 hours 75 minutes

75 min = 60 min + 15 min

= 1 hr + 15 min

↗

carry 1

↘

9 hr 75 min = 9 hr + 1 hr + 15 min

= $\boxed{10 \text{ hr } 15 \text{ min}}$

35   96 hours = how many days?

There are 24 hours in a day.

So divide: $\dfrac{96}{24}$ = number of days

$\begin{array}{r} 4 \\ 24)\overline{96} \\ \underline{96} \\ 0 \end{array}$ $\boxed{4 \text{ days}}$

36 $\overset{1\ 0\ 4\ 9}{2\cancel{1}\cancel{5}.\cancel{0}0}$
$\underline{-117.81}$
$\boxed{97.19}$

37

$$72$$
$$\times\ _1 35$$
$$\overline{_1}$$
$$360 \leftarrow \text{(multiply } 72 \times 5 \text{ firs} \times$$
$$\underline{+\ 216\!\downarrow} \leftarrow \text{(multiply } 72 \times 3 \text{ sec} \times \text{d—then move over one place)}$$
$$\boxed{2{,}520}$$
$$\nwarrow \text{ (add)}$$

38

$$\frac{6}{15}$$

$$-\ \frac{2}{15}$$

$$\overline{}$$

$$\frac{4}{\boxed{15}}$$

(subtract numerators [6 − 2 = 4]
when denominators are *same*;
keep same denominator)

39

$$\begin{array}{r} 21 \\ 33\overline{)693} \\ 66 \\ \overline{33} \end{array} \qquad \boxed{21}$$

40

$$\frac{1}{4} \times \frac{1}{2} = \frac{1 \times 1}{4 \times 2} = \boxed{\frac{1}{8}}$$

(multiply numerators)

(multiply denominators)

41 $\dfrac{7}{10} = 7 \times \dfrac{1}{10}$

$\dfrac{1}{10} = .1$, so $\dfrac{7}{10} = 7 \times .1 = \boxed{.7}$

$\uparrow \qquad \uparrow$

(one decimal place to left)

42 $\dfrac{2}{3}$ of $9 = \dfrac{2}{3} \times 9 = \dfrac{2}{3} \times \dfrac{9}{1}$

Reduce:

$$\frac{2}{\underset{1}{\cancel{3}}} \times \frac{\overset{3}{\cancel{9}}}{1}$$

$$\frac{2}{1} \times \frac{3}{1} = \frac{6}{1} = \boxed{6}$$

43 $24 \times 30 =$
$$\begin{array}{r} 24 \\ \times\ {}_1 30 \\ \hline 720 \end{array}$$

$24 \times 3 =$
$$\begin{array}{r} 24 \\ \times\ {}_1 3 \\ \hline 72 \end{array}$$

$(24 \times 30) - (24 \times 3)$
$$\downarrow$$
$720 \quad -72 =$
$$\begin{array}{r} 720 \\ -\ 72 \\ \hline \end{array}$$

$$\begin{array}{r} {}^{61}\\ 7\!\!\!/20 \\ -\ 72 \\ \hline \boxed{648} \end{array}$$

44 $\overset{\Large .}{}$ ← (keep decimal right above decimal below)
$$5\overline{)15.05}$$

$$\begin{array}{r} 3.01 \\ 5\overline{)15.05} \\ 15\downarrow \\ \hline 00 \\ 0\downarrow \\ \hline 5 \end{array} \qquad \boxed{3.01}$$

45 $\dfrac{4}{9} = \dfrac{\square}{36}$

$\dfrac{4}{9} \times \dfrac{4}{4} = \dfrac{16}{36}$ ← $\boxed{?=16}$

46 $100\,\text{cm} = 1\,\text{m (meter)}$

$300\,\text{cm} = 3\,\text{m}$

$3\,\text{cm} = \dfrac{3}{100}\,\text{m} = .03\,\text{meters}$

$303\,\text{cm} = 3.03\,\text{m}$

So $707\,\text{cm} = 7.07\,\text{m}$

$$\begin{array}{r} 3.03 \\ +\ 7.07 \\ \hline \end{array} \qquad\qquad \begin{array}{r} {}^{1} \\ 3.03 \\ +\ 7.07 \\ \hline 10.10 \text{ or } \boxed{10.1\,\text{m}} \end{array}$$

47   8.4   Note: There are a sum total of

$\times$ 7.6 $\underline{2}$ decimal places to the left

so you will have 2 decimal

places to the left in your answer.

$$\begin{array}{r} 8.4 \\ \times\ 7.6 \\ \hline {}_1 504 \\ 588 \\ \hline \boxed{63.84} \end{array}$$

48   4 hours 30 minutes

$\times$ 3   (multiply the 3 by the 4 hours

    <u>and</u> the 30 minutes

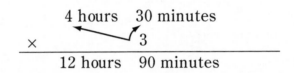

    4 hours   30 minutes

$\times$ 3

$\overline{}$ 12 hours   90 minutes

90 minutes = 60 minutes + 30 minutes

= 1 hour + 30 minutes

So

12 hours + 90 minutes =

12 hours + 1 hour + 30 minutes =

$\boxed{\text{13 hours 30 minutes}}$

49 $5\dfrac{1}{3} \times 3\dfrac{1}{8} =$

    $\downarrow$ $\downarrow$ Express mixed fractions

    as single fractions :

$\dfrac{16}{3} \times \dfrac{25}{8}$ $5\dfrac{1}{3} = \dfrac{(5\times3)+1}{3} = \dfrac{16}{3}$

Cancel, reduce : $3\dfrac{1}{8} = \dfrac{(3\times8)+1}{8} = \dfrac{25}{8}$

$\dfrac{\overset{2}{\cancel{16}}}{3} \times \dfrac{25}{\cancel{8}} =$

$\dfrac{2\times25}{3} = \boxed{\dfrac{50}{3}}$ or $\boxed{16\dfrac{2}{3}}$

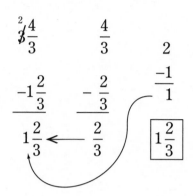

50

$3\dfrac{1}{3}$ $\dfrac{1}{3}-\dfrac{2}{3}$ doesn't go, so

$-1\dfrac{2}{3}$ add 1 to $\dfrac{1}{3}$ to get $\dfrac{4}{3}$.

Borrow 1 from 3.

$\overset{2}{\cancel{3}}\dfrac{4}{3}$ $\dfrac{4}{3}$ 2

$-1\dfrac{2}{3}$ $-\dfrac{2}{3}$ $\dfrac{-1}{1}$

$1\dfrac{2}{3} \leftarrow$ $\dfrac{2}{3}$ $\boxed{1\dfrac{2}{3}}$

Appendix A: Hot Prefixes and Roots

Here is a list of the most important prefixes and roots which impart a certain feeling or meaning—they can be instant clues to the meanings of more than 125,000 words.

PREFIXES THAT MEAN *TO, WITH, BETWEEN, OR AMONG*

PREFIX	MEANING	EXAMPLES
ad, ac, af, an, ap, ap, as, at	to, toward	adapt—to fit into adhere—to stick to attract—to draw near
com, con, co, col	with, together	combine—to bring together contact—to touch together collect—to bring together co-worker—one who works together with another worker
in, il, ir, im	into	inject—to put into impose—to force into illustrate—to put into example irritate—to put into discomfort
inter	between, among	international—among nations interact—to act among the people
pro	forward, going ahead	proceed—to go forward promote—to move forward

PREFIXES THAT MEAN *BAD*

PREFIX	MEANING	EXAMPLES
mal	wrong, bad	malady—illness malevolent—bad malfunction—bad functioning
mis	wrong, badly	mistreat—to treat badly mistake—to get wrong

PREFIXES THAT MEAN *AWAY FROM, NOT,* OR *AGAINST*

PREFIX	MEANING	EXAMPLES
ab	away from	absent—not to be present, away abscond—to run away
de, dis	away from, down, the opposite of, apart, not	depart—to go away from decline—to turn down dislike—not to like dishonest—not honest distant—apart
ex, e, ef	out, from	exit—to go out eject—to throw out efface—to rub out, erase
in, il, ir, im	not	inactive—not active impossible—not possible ill-mannered—not mannered irreversible—not reversible
non	not	nonsense—no sense nonstop—having no stops
un	not	unhelpful—not helpful uninterested—not interested
anti	against	anti-freeze—a substance used to prevent freezing anti-social—refers to someone who's not social
ob	against, in front of	obstacle—something that stands in the way of obstinate—inflexible

PREFIXES THAT DENOTE DISTANCE

PREFIX	MEANING	EXAMPLES
circum	around	circumscribe—to write or inscribe in a circle circumspect—to watch around or be very careful
equ, equi	equal, the same	equalize—to make equal equitable—fair, equal
post	after	postpone—to do after postmortem—after death
pre	before	preview—a viewing that goes before another viewing prehistorical—before written history
trans	across	transcontinental—across the continent transit—act of going across
re	back, again	retell—to tell again recall—to call back, to remember
sub	under	subordinate—under something else subconscious—under the conscious
super	over, above	superimpose—to put something over something else superstar—a star greater than other stars
un, uni	one	unity—oneness unanimous—sharing one view unidirectional—having one direction

ROOTS

ROOT	MEANING	EXAMPLES
cap, capt, cept, ceive	to take, to hold	captive—one who is held receive—to take capable—to be able to take hold of things concept—an idea or thought held in mind
cred	to believe	credible—believable credit—belief, trust
curr, curs, cours	to run	current—now in progress, running cursor—a moveable indicator recourse—to run for aid
dic, dict	to say	indicate—to say by demonstrating diction—verbal saying
duc, duct	to lead	induce—to lead to action aqueduct—a pipe or waterway that leads water somewhere
fac, fic, fect, fy	to make, to do	facile—easy to do fiction—something that has been made up satisfy—to make happy affect—to make a change in
jec, ject	to throw	project—to put forward trajectory—a path of an object that has been thrown
mit, mis	to send	admit—to send in missile—something that gets sent through the air
pon, pos	to place	transpose—to place across compose—to put into place many parts deposit—to place in something
scrib, script	to write	describe—to write or tell about scripture—a written tablet

spec, spic	to look	specimen—an example to look at inspect—to look over
ten, tain	to hold	maintain—to hold up or keep retentive—holding
ven, vent	to come	advent—a coming convene—to come together

Appendix B: The Dangers of National School Entrance Testing

Are the national testing companies—which test hundreds of thousands of students each year—actually destroying our kids' potential and enthusiasm for learning? This book develops and restores that potential and passion, allowing the student to score markedly higher even though the tests may be flawed.

Here is a question on an actual Secondary School Admission test (SSAT), the test for private high school entrance. This question has also appeared in the company's official test-preparation guide for more than ten years. It is one of many questions with such ambiguities.

See if you or your child can correctly answer this question.

> What is the meaning of the word POLISH?
>
> (A) burnish (B) lighten (C) wax (D) coat (E) clean

The correct answer (according to the testing company) is (A) burnish.
But POLISH as can be seen in any dictionary to mean smooth, brighten, or refine, making all the choices correct!

The Dangers of Ambiguity

When a student who is already anxious about taking a test attempts to answer not one but a series of questions that have ambiguous answers or cannot be answered, the student will get so befuddled that he will do poorly on the rest of the test. However, if a student is armed with the strategies in this book, his confidence will be so heightened that he will see through these flaws and not get discouraged.

Here are some of the erroneous questions that have appeared on the actual SSAT and are also in the official book of the *SSAT, SSAT: Preparing and Applying*. These are taken directly from the Upper Level Practice Test II.

> Find the meaning of:
>
> 28. ANDROGYNOUS
>   (A) alien
>   (B) bisexual
>   (C) metallic
>   (D) underground
>   (E) insecticide
>
> SSAT Answer: B

The definition of androgynous is both male and female in one, not necessarily bisexual!

> 49. Anesthesiologist is to sedate as
>   (A) optometrist is to glasses
>   (B) hypnotist is to spell
>   (C) agronomist is to plant
>   (D) economist is to prediction
>   (E) humanist is to people
>
> SSAT Answer: B

Any person who knows even little about analogies would answer this one as follows: "The purpose of an anesthesiologist is to sedate as the purpose of a hypnotist is to spell?" It is elementary to realize that "sedate" should not have been used as a verb. In fact, the phrase "is to" in the stem of the question (sedate) has to be the same part of speech as all the words in the choices. Note that in Choice A, *glasses* is a noun, in Choice B *spell* is a noun after "is to" , in Choice C *plant* is a verb, and the word after "is to" in the choices D and E are nouns. This is a totally erroneous analogy question.

45. Happy is to worried as

    (A) please is to passion

    (B) ecstatic is to panicked

    (C) cheerful is to confused

    (D) glow is to glare

    (E) lively is to dull

SSAT Answer: B

Here the test writer used the following: Happy is to ecstatic as worried is to panicked. The sequence is incorrect for analogies. The question stem should have been "Happy is to ecstatic" and the correct choice should have been (B) worried is to panicked.

3. PREVALENT

    (A) ahead

    (B) common

    (C) elected

    (D) overlooked

    (E) collected

SSAT Answer: B

Prevalent is defined as "widely existent," or "generally accepted."
"Common" does not fit.

1. PATHETIC

    (A) guidance

    (B) trash

    (C) poor

    (D) direction

    (E) wretched

SSAT Answer: E

PATHETIC is an adjective. Choices A and D are nouns, and Choice B is either a verb or noun. Choices A, D, and B must be modified.

Actual SSAT Questions

Here are actual SSAT questions that many people have asked me how to solve because they thought they were too difficult and felt it was unfair of the testing company to use them. These questions are not ambiguous, but there are powerful strategies you can use to answer each question. Learning these strategies—all of which appear in this book—will give your child the confidence to get through the test no matter what the test is like, leveling the playing field for everyone.

Find the closest meaning to the word in capitalized letters:

1. Q. DECEIVE: (A) alter (B) examine (C) astonish (D) mislead (E) pretend

   A. (D) See Appendix A—these prefixes and roots will give you the meaning of more than 150,000 words! Since the prefix DE means "away from," it is negative. So let's look for a choice that gives the feeling of being negative. The only choice is (D) mislead, since the prefix MIS is also negative. (See Vocabulary Strategy 1.)

(For the following vocabulary questions, strategies and additional examples can be found in Vocabulary Strategies 1 and 2.)

2. Q. COMPASSION: (A) sympathy (B) honor (C) shyness (D) amazement (E) courage

   A. (A) Associate words with other words—another strategy you should have learned in this book. Look for some part of the word that you understand. You've heard of PASSION. Now look for a choice that has some emotion in it. Choice A is the best one.

3. Q. REMINISCENCE: (A) limitation (B) contraction (C) moderation (D) recollection (E) removal

   A. (D) What word seems to be part of or associated with REMINISCENCE? REMIND. Choice D is the best one.

4. Q. PROPHESY: (A) defeat (B) annoy (C) foretell (D) testify (E) prompt

   A. (C) Look for the prefix to give a clue: PRO, which means "forward" or "ahead." Which choice looks like it means something forward? (C) foretell.

5. Q. ASCERTAIN: (A) give up (B) add to (C) join with (D) follow after (E) find out

   A. (E) What word in ASCERTAIN do you recognize? CERTAIN. So look for a choice that is associated closely with the word CERTAIN. Wouldn't it be (E) find out?

6. Q. RESIDUAL: (A) surrounded by (B) leftover (C) responsive to (D) finished (E) runaway

   A. (B) The prefix RE means "back." What choice has something to do with "back?" (B) leftover.

7. Q. ADJUNCT: (A) endeavor (B) impatience (C) ridicule (D) compulsion (E) accessory

   A. (E) The prefix AD means "toward" or "to." What does JUNCT make you think of? Perhaps JUNCTION or JOIN? What joins something? (E) accessory

8. Q. ENTOURAGE: (A) attendants (B) journeys (C) schedules (D) displays (E) awards

   A. (A) This is a difficult one to figure out, but think of TOUR in ENTOURAGE. So you can eliminate choices D and E. You are left to choose either A, B or C, and now your chances of getting it correct are one in three, which is better than one in five. (The correct answer is (A) attendants.)

9. Q. IMPASSE (A) deadlock (B) distortion (C) variance (D) neutrality (E) recklessness

   A. (A) The prefix IM usually means "not." Look at the word PASS in IMPASSE. You can figure out that the word might mean "not to be able to pass." So look for a word that means to "stop" or "prevent from passing." You can see that (A) deadlock fits the bill.

Let's look at some analogies. (For the following analogies, strategies and additional examples can be found in Analogies.)

10. Q. Immaculate is to dirt as
       (A) indecent is to person
       (B) inclement is to rain
       (C) immortal is to heaven
       (D) impious is to volume
       (E) innocent is to guilt

    A. (E) Let's say you don't know what the meaning of "immaculate" is. Since it must relate to "dirt," let's take a guess and say "immaculate" may mean "not dirty." So let's see if we can find an opposite in the choices. Choice E is the only one.

11. Q. Intangible is to touching as
       (A) incisive is to cutting
       (B) inadvertent is to seeing
       (C) inaudible is to hearing
       (D) inarticulate is to reading
       (E) incendiary is to burning

    A. (C) Just as in the answer to the first question, if you don't know the meaning of intangible, you could think of it as an opposite to touching and see if you get an opposite in one of the choices. Choice C looks like the one.

12. Q. Map is to land as
       (A) negative is to print
       (B) diagram is to machine
       (C) camera is to film
       (D) crayon is to paint
       (E) lens is to glass

    A. Let's get a meaningful sentence that relates map and land. (This is a powerful strategy for cracking analogies.) You can say a map tells you how to get around the land. Now look for a choice that, when you put the words of the choice in the same sentence form, you get a match.
    Look at Choice A: a negative tells you how to get around a print. No.
    Look at Choice B: a diagram tells you how to get around a machine. Possible.
    Look at Choice C: a camera tells you how to get around a film. No.
    Look at Choice D: a crayon tells you how to get around a paint. No.
    Look at Choice E: a lens tells you how to get around a glass. No.
    Choice B is best.

13. Q. Recalcitrant is to obedience as insolent is to
    (A) luck
    (B) stealth
    (C) fear
    (D) respect
    (E) anger

    A. (D) Since the "Re" in "Recalcitrant" means "back," it has a negative connotation, so let's assume that "recalcitrant" means the opposite of "obedience." Now let's look for an opposite to "insolent." Let's assume that the "in" means "not" and the word is negative. So look for a positive choice that somewhat relates to behavior. It is Choice D.

14. Q. Obsessed is to interested as
    (A) weak is to ill
    (B) ferocious is to unexpected
    (C) pristine is to clean
    (D) moist is to humid
    (E) fashionable is to new

    A. (C) What could the word "obsessed" mean if it is related in some way to the word "interested?" Let's say it is a level of how interested you are. Let's assume that level is "very" interested. Notice that Choices A, B, D, and E do not have this relation. So even if you didn't know that the word "pristine" meant "very clean," you still could have eliminated all the other choices to get Choice C.

15. Q. Variegated is to color as
    (A) polymorphous is to shape
    (B) amorphous is to skeleton
    (C) quadrilateral is to polygon
    (D) aeronautic is to plane
    (E) celestial is to planet

    A. (A) Even if you don't know the meaning of "variegated," you can associate "vary" with that word. So if things are varied, there are many colors. Let's look for a choice that shows many of something else. "Poly" means many, so (A) is the best choice.

Math—All of these questions can be answered quickly using the powerful strategies in this book.

16. Q. Of the following, 0.49 × 81 is closest to
    (A) $\frac{1}{2}$ of 80
    (B) $\frac{1}{2}$ of 90
    (C) $\frac{1}{4}$ of 80
    (D) $\frac{1}{4}$ of 90
    (E) 4 times 80

    A. (A) The key word here is "closest to." So instead of multiplying 0.49 × 81, let's approximate 0.49 to 0.5—which is $\frac{1}{2}$—and 81 to 80. Thus you can see that Choice A is correct. (See Math Strategy 3.)

17. Q. All of the following are greater than $\frac{1}{2}$ EXCEPT
    (A) $\frac{101}{200}$
    (B) $\frac{17}{33}$
    (C) $\frac{7}{12}$
    (D) $\frac{600}{1000}$
    (E) $\frac{24}{50}$

A. (E) Whenever you have to test all the choices, start with Choice E. You should immediately connect $\frac{1}{2}$ with $^{24}/_{50}$. $\frac{1}{2} = {}^{25}/_{50}$, so you can see that the quantity in Choice E is less than $\frac{1}{2}$. (See Math Strategy 5.)

18. Q. For what price is 20 percent off the same as $20 off?
 (A) $1
 (B) $10
 (C) $100
 (D) $1,000
 (E) It is never the same.

A. (C) Try the choices, starting with Choice D. 20% of $1,000 is $200. $200 off $1,000 gives you $800. For Choice D, $20 off $1,000 is $980. Look at Choice C: 20% of $100 is $20. 20% of $100 is $80. For Choice C, $20 off $100 is also $80. Thus Choice C is correct. (See Math Strategies 5 and 2.)

19. Q. If $\frac{1}{4}$ N = 12, then $\frac{1}{2}$ N =
 (A) 3
 (B) 6
 (C) 24
 (D) 48
 (E) 96

A. (C) How do I relate $\frac{1}{4}$ with $\frac{1}{2}$? $\frac{1}{4} = \frac{1}{2} \times \frac{1}{2}$. So $\frac{1}{4}$ N = $\frac{1}{2} \times \frac{1}{2}$ N = 12.
Multiply by 2 and we get: $2 \times \frac{1}{2} \times \frac{1}{2}$ N = $2 \times 12 = 24$. (See Math Strategy 1.)

20. Q. Of the following, 15 percent of $8.95 is closest to
 (A) $1.95
 (B) $1.75
 (C) $1.50
 (D) $1.35
 (E) $1.00

A. (D) Look at the key word "closest." Round up $8.95 to $9.00. Remember that 15% of a quantity is 10% of the quantity + 1/2 that result. So 15% of $9 is 10% of $9, which equals $0.90, then + $\frac{1}{2}$ of that amount, which is $\frac{1}{2} + 0.90 = 0.45$. So the result is $1.35. This is a good way to figure out a 15% tip at a restaurant! (See Math Strategies 2 and 3.)

21. Q. John has x dollars. Ann has $5 more than John. If Ann gives John $10, then, in terms of x, how many dollars will Ann have?
 (A) x – 15
 (B) x – 10
 (C) x – 5
 (D) x + 5
 (E) x + 15

A. (C) Translate verbal to math. Let J = x. "Has" translates to =, "more" translates to +. Therefore, "Ann has $5 more than John" translates to A = 5 + J. If Ann gives John $10, Ann has A–10. Since A = 5 + J, A – 10 = 5 + J – 10.
A –10 = J – 5 = x – 5 (See Math Strategy 2.)

22. Q. A store regularly sells books at 20% off the list price. At a sale its regular prices are reduced 10 percent. The sale price is what percent of the list price?
  (A) 30%
  (B) 70%
  (C) 72%
  (D) 79%
  (E) 85%

A. (C) Imagine an item at the bookstore that costs an even $100. 20% off $100 gives you $80, and thus the price of the item is $80. Since at a sale the store's regular price is reduced 10%, let's take 10% off $80. That gives $8. So the final price is $80 − $8 = $72. The question asks: the sale price is what percent of the list price. We had calculated that the sale price is $72. The list price is $100. Translate "is" to =, "what" to x, "percent" to /100, and "of" to × (times).

The sale price	is	what	percent	of	list price
$72	=	x	/100	×	$100

Thus $72 = x/100 \times (100) = x$, so $x = 72$. (See Math Strategy 2.)

Appendix C: How Will Your Child Do on The Actual SAT Test When He or She is in High School?

This test is based on Dr. Gruber's following students who he has worked personally with from 3rd Grade through High School. He has tabulated what scores they received on his tests in 3rd Grade, 6th Grade and so on to the scores they receive on their SAT in High School.

As an example, this test- 20 question-30 minute Math Test and 22 question -22 minute Verbal Test will tell you what potential the student has for doing well on the SAT test when they are a junior or senior in high school. By learning the strategies and methods in this test and internalizing them throughout the student's career, they will perform remarkably well later on the actual SAT.

Thus if the score is low on this test, don't worry! By learning and internalizing these methods, the student should vastly increase his or her score by the time he or she actually gets to taking the actual SAT.

ANSWER SHEET

Complete Mark ●   **Examples of Incomplete Marks** ◐ ⊗ ⊖ ◔ ⊘ ◖ ◑ ◕

READING

	A	B	C	D			A	B	C	D
1	○	○	○	○		4	○	○	○	○
2	○	○	○	○		5	○	○	○	○
3	○	○	○	○						

WRITING AND LANGUAGE

	A	B	C	D			A	B	C	D
1	○	○	○	○		4	○	○	○	○
2	○	○	○	○		5	○	○	○	○
3	○	○	○	○						

MATH

	A	B	C	D			A	B	C	D
1	○	○	○	○		6	○	○	○	○
2	○	○	○	○		7	○	○	○	○
3	○	○	○	○		8	○	○	○	○
4	○	○	○	○		9	○	○	○	○
5	○	○	○	○		10	○	○	○	○

PART 1: READING

8 Minutes

Read the following passage and answer the questions.

The school principal was offering a gold pen to anyone who could drop an egg from the roof of the school without the egg breaking. Sally made a parachute from an old cloth and tied the cloth to a plastic cup. To pro-
5 tect the egg from hard knocks, she lined the cup with cotton balls, putting the egg inside the cup. Everybody made some sort of contraption, but Sally's was by far the most interesting and promising. Everybody dropped their egg-contraption. When Sally dropped hers, there
10 was a strong breeze at the time, but the parachute opened smoothly. A little ways down, however, the plastic cup turned upside down and the egg fell out and broke on the ground. Although nobody won the prize, Sally had realized how to improve on her contraption,
15 was excited to try again, and was determined that she would win the prize the next try.

Questions

1. Which is the best title for the story?

   (A) "The Gold Pen"
   (B) "A Strange Contest"
   (C) "Sally's Parachute"
   (D) The Strong Breeze"

2. What could have made the cup turn over?

   (A) too small an egg
   (B) possible collapse of the parachute
   (C) the wind
   (D) cotton balls in the wrong place in the cup

3. What was Sally's feeling after her egg broke on the ground?

   (A) surprise
   (B) anger
   (C) sadness
   (D) encouragement

4. What prize was being offered to the winner?

   (A) an egg
   (B) a new cloth
   (C) a parachute
   (D) a pen

5. The word "promising" in the third paragraph of the story refers to

   (A) the principal guaranteeing the winner of the golden pen
   (B) the feeling that nobody would win the prize
   (C) the likelihood that Sally's parachute invention would win the prize.
   (D) Sally's determination to win

6. Which is an assumption and not a fact in the story?

   (A) The principal was offering a golden pen to the winner.
   (B) The feeling that anyone could win the prize.
   (C) There was a strong breeze when Sally dropped her egg.
   (D) Sally would win the contest on the next try.

PART 2: WRITING

6 Minutes

In each of the following sentences there may be an error in wording. If there is an error, choose the underlined part that should be changed in order to make the sentence correct. No sentence has more than one error, and some have none. If there is no error, choose D.

Example:

They is coming to the party tomorrow night. No error.
   A B   C   D

Here you would choose A, since the underlined word marked A is incorrect.

1. Of all my three brothers, John is the worse soccer
  A   B C

  player. No error.
         D

2. Sam dropped his money on the sidewalk; however,
          A

  when he looked for it, he couldn't find it nowhere.
                         B   C

  No error.
   D

3. The coins were so strange that we couldn't decide
           A   B

  where it came from. No error.
      C   D

4. You will see not only a beautiful sunset and also
    A   B   C

  see a gorgeous sunrise. No error.
               D

5. John was sure that he has arrived at school on time,
          A B

  but it appeared that he was late. No error.
      C   D

6. Some things should be read carefully, others less
          A

  carefully, and still others not at all. No error.
        B   C   D

PART 3: VOCABULARY

8 Minutes

Choose the best answer from the choices.

1. The meaning of PREVIEW is

   (A) to show
   (B) to see before
   (C) to gather
   (D) to get into one group

2. The meaning of MALADY is

   (A) female person
   (B) puzzle
   (C) sickness
   (D) helper

3. The meaning of THERMAL is

   (A) dangerous
   (B) wild
   (C) dark
   (D) heat-related

4. The meaning of INTRANSIGENT (hint: use the prefix "in" as not) is

   (A) noisy
   (B) difficult
   (C) not compromising
   (D) not able to swim

5. The meaning of DELUDE is

   (A) to watch
   (B) to help
   (C) to see
   (D) to fool

6. Which words contain the same prefix? (i) misnomer (ii) mislead (iii) missle (iv) mystify

   (A) i ,ii,iii only
   (B) i, ii, iii, iv
   (C) i, ii only
   (D) ii only

7. If the root GEN means animal or of an animal type, the meaning of PROGENY could be

   (A) son or daughter
   (B) stable
   (C) zoo
   (D) habitat

8. Which is not always or not mostly true: The prefix

   (A) PRO means forward
   (B) RE means back
   (C) ANTI means against
   (D) IN means not

9. If the prefix CIRCUM means around and VEN means to go, then the OPPOSITE of CIRCUM-VENT means

   (A) to watch closely
   (B) to go quickly
   (C) to go immediately
   (D) to go in a direct manner

10. Which of the following words impart a "bad" or "negative" meaning? For example, HORRIBLE imparts a "bad" meaning because a part of the word, HOR means "tremble."

   (A) appease
   (B) munificence
   (C) fortitude
   (D) detriment

PART 4: MATH

30 Minutes

1. 13/25 is what percent?

   (A) 50
   (B) 51
   (C) 52
   (D) 53

2. In the subtraction problem, 205 − 99, it is easiest to do which of the following?

   (A) 205 − 99
   (B) 204 − 100
   (C) 206 − 100
   (D) 205 − 100 = 105 + 1

3. Find: 3 hours   20 minutes
       +   4 hours   70 minutes

   (A) 8 hours
   (B) 8 hours 20minutes
   (C) 8 hours 30 minutes
   (D) 8 hours 40 minutes

4. $5\frac{1}{2} \times 3\frac{1}{2} =$

   (A) 8 ¼
   (B) 15 ¼
   (C) 15 ½
   (D) 19 ¼

5. John has 24 baseball cards. He gives 10 of them to Mary and 4 more to Harry. If he sells the remainder of them for 5 cents each, how much money does he receive?

   (A) 50 cents
   (B) 60 cents
   (C) 70 cents
   (D) 80 cents

6. 1/2 cup of water is mixed with 2/3 cups of orange juice to make orangeade. How many cups of orangeade are made?

   (A) 1 cup
   (B) 1 1/6 cups

   (C) 1 1/4 cups
   (D) 1 1/2 cups

7. Without a calculator, one step in the process of the easiest way to figure out *what is 25% of 160* would be to

   (A) multiply 25 × 160
   (B) reduce 25% to its equivalent fraction
   (C) double 25 and half 160
   (D) change 25% to the decimal 0.25 and then multiply this decimal by 160

8. Harry has $15. He gives Mary $10 and Mary gives Paul $5. Paul then gives Harry $2. How much does Harry now have?

   (A) $14
   (B) $12
   (C) $7
   (D) $2

9. To find out the closest approximation to 8. 1 × 8.9, you would do which of the following if you are given the choices to be either 60,70 80, 90 or 100.

   (A) I would multiply 8.1 × 8.9, then round off
   (B) I would multiply 8 × 8.9 or 8.1 × 9 then round off
   (C) I would multiply 8 × 9 then round off
   (D) I would divide the choices 60,70,80,90,100 by 8.9 and see which one gives me 8.1

10. An odd number times an odd number then added to an even number gives me

   (A) an odd number
   (B) an even number
   (C) 0
   (D) either an even or an odd number

11. 2/3 of a number is 6. The number is

   (A) 7
   (B) 8
   (C) 9
   (D) 10

12. The hand of the clock to the right goes from 0 to 1, 1 to 2, 2 to 3, 3 to 0, 0 to 1, and so forth. Every time it goes from quarter to the next (that is from 0 to 1, from 1 to 2, etc.) a dollar comes out of the clock. If the hand starts at 0 and travels around so that $173 dollars come out of the clock, where is the hand pointing as the 173rd dollar comes out?

(A) 0
(B) 1
(C) 2
(D) 3

13. 5 is what percent of 10?

(A) 20
(B) 40
(C) 50
(D) 60

14. A recipe calls for 1 cup of sugar to 6 cups of water. How much water is needed for 2 ½ cups of sugar?

(A) 10
(B) 15
(C) 20
(D) 25

15. What is the area of the shaded region if the area of the small circle is 12 and the area of the large circle is 20?

(A) 32
(B) 8
(C) 10
(D) cannot tell

16. In the figure below, CD and BC are the same length. ED and AE are also the same length. What is the perimeter of the figure?

(A) 27
(B) 32
(C) 35
(D) 40

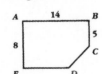

17. The bar graph below describes the cost of various items used in a particular recipe. What item costs approximately 60 percent of the total cost for all of the items?

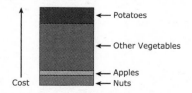

(A) nuts
(B) apples
(C) potatoes
(D) other vegetables

The following two questions refer to the graph below.

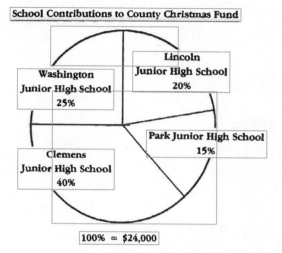

18. The contribution from Washington Junior High School was what part of the contributions from the other schools?

(A) 1/2
(B) 1/3
(C) 1/4
(D) 1/5

19. What contribution did Lincoln Junior High School make?

(A) $24,000
(B) $12,000
(C) $6,400
(D) $4,800

20. There are 24 girls at a party. The ratio of boys to girls at the party is 3 to 4. How many boys are there at the party?

(A) 12
(B) 18
(C) 28
(D) 36

ANSWERS AND SCORING

Answers

Reading

1. C
2. C
3. D
4. D
5. C
6. D

Writing

1. C
2. C
3. C
4. C
5. B
6. D

Vocabulary

1. B
2. C
3. D
4. C
5. D
6. C
7. A

8. D
9. D
10 D

Math

1. C
2. C or D
3. C
4. D
5. A
6. B
7. B
8. C
9. C
10. A
11. C
12. B
13. C
14. B
15. B
16. D
17. D
18. B
19. D
20. B

Approximate SAT Scoring

Verbal—Reading, Writing
0–6 200
7–9....300
10–11....400
12–13....500
14–16....600
17–19....700
20–21....750
22...800

Math
0–6 200
7–9....300
10–12....400
13–14....500
15–16....600
17–18....700
19....750
20....800

EXPLANATORY ANSWERS

Reading

1. (C) The story really describes the cleverness of Sally's parachute.

   This idea is present everywhere in the story and is the main theme of the story.

   Wrong Choices:

   (A) The Gold Pen only occurs marginally at the beginning of the story and end of the story and is not the focus of interest throughout the story.

   (B) Certainly this was a strange contest, but that is not the chief element in the story—it is the parachute contraption that gets our interest.

   (D) The strong breeze only occurred in one part of the story and although it might have been the cause of the cup turning, it is not the main attraction or theme of the story.

2. (C) Look at the wording in the story: "When Sally dropped hers, there was <u>a strong breeze at the time</u>, but the parachute opened smoothly. A little ways down, <u>however</u>, the plastic cup turned upside down..." The word <u>however</u> tells us that even though the parachute opened smoothly, the breeze later affected the cup.

   Wrong Choices:

   (A) Too small an egg would not make the cup turn over.

   (B) The parachute opened smoothly but even if the parachute collapsed, due to the wind, it wouldn't make the cup turn over. It would just make the cup go down faster.

   (D) Cotton balls are so light that even if they were in the wrong place in the cup, they would not make the cup turn over.

3. (D) After her egg broke, the story says (in the last paragraph), Sally realized how to improve her contraption, and was excited to try again. She was also determined that she would win on the next try. This all indicates <u>encouragement</u>, not (A) surprise, or (B) anger or (C) sadness.

4. (D) The beginning of the story says that the principal was offering a <u>gold pen</u> to the winner.

   Wrong Choices:

   (A) Although students were dropping eggs, that wasn't the prize.

   (B) Although Sally used an old cloth for her parachute, that wasn't the prize.

   (C) Although Sally made a parachute, that wasn't the prize.

   Note that Choices A, B, and C try to lure the student who has superficially read the passage and casually just caught the words egg, cloth, parachute in the passage.

5. (C) Look at the third paragraph. It says that "Sally's was by far the most interesting and <u>promising</u>." This refers to Sally's parachute contraption. Although the word <u>promising</u> can generally refer to Choices A, B, and D also, the word <u>promising</u> *in the third paragraph* cannot. Therefore Choices A, B, and D are incorrect.

6. (D) Although Sally was determined that she would win on the next try (last paragraph), this is an *assumption* and *not a fact*. Thus Choice D is correct.

   Wrong Choices:

   (A) It is a *fact* that the principal was offering a golden pen to the winner (beginning).

(B) It is a *fact* that nobody won the prize (see last paragraph).

(C) It is a *fact* that there was a strong breeze when Sally dropped her egg (see third paragraph).

You should realize that in many of these questions you have to be very exact in your analysis. You cannot base answers on your own assumptions or feelings, but must base them on what is in the story. For example, in question 3, although your feeling might have been one of anger when the egg broke, this was not Sally's feeling. And it is *Sally's feeling* that is asked for in the question.

Writing

1. (C)". . . John is the <u>worst</u> soccer player."

2. (C) ". . . he couldn't find it <u>anywhere</u>."

3. (C) ". . . we couldn't decide where <u>they</u> came from" (they refers to coins).

4. (C) "You will see not only a beautiful sunset, <u>but</u> also see . . ."

5. (B) "John was so sure that he <u>had</u> arrived at school on time . . ." Use had to indicate the past of <u>was</u>.

6. (D) No error.

Vocabulary—Associate parts of words with prefixes or roots of words

1. (B) Think of PRE meaning "before." Other words are predict, precursor, preceding.

2. (C) Think of MAL as "bad". Other words are malevolent, malfunction, malware.

3. (D) Associate THERM with "Thermometer." A thermometer measures heat.

4. (C) Think of the part TRANS meaning across as in transport or trans-continental. If you think IN mean "not" it seems that INTRANIGENT means that you can't get something across. The closest choice is "not giving in" or "not compromising".

5. (D) DE means "against" "away from". LUD means to play. So DELUDE means to "play against". The closest choice is D.

6. (C) The prefix in "misnomer" is "mis". The prefix in "mislead" is "mis". "Missle" and "Mystify" have no real prefix.

7. (A) Since PRO means forward or something that goes first, a "daughter" or "son" would fit.

8. (D) Choices A,B,C are always the case. However, IN can mean "not" as in INDECISIVE (not decisive) or "in" as in INJECT "throw in".

9. (D) Since CIRCUMVENT means to come around, not go directly, Choice D is the best one.

10. (D) The prefix "de" mans away or against, so Choice D would be the best fit.

Math

1. (C) Use the strategy of multiplying the numerator and denominator by the same number to get a percent.
$$\frac{13}{25} \times \frac{4}{4} = \frac{52}{100} = \mathbf{52\%}$$

2. (C) or (D) Make it easy for yourself by working with simple numbers. $205 - 99$ is the same as $206 - 100$ since you're adding 1 to both amounts here. Thus C is correct. Since 99 is $100 - 1$, $205 - 99$ is the same as $205 - 100 + 1$ which is the same as Choice D.

3. (C) 3 hours + 4 hours = 7 hours. 20 minutes + 70 minutes = 90 minutes. So 7 hours + 90 minutes is your answer. There is no choice for that so we have to write 90 minutes in a different form. Write 90 minutes as 30 minutes + 60 minutes which is equal to 30 minutes + 1 hr. Thus 7 hours + 90 minutes = 8 hrs + 30 minutes.

4. (D) Write 5 ½ and 3 ½ in a different form. $5\ 1/2 = 11/2$; $3\ 1/2 = 7/2$. Thus $5\ 1/2 \times 3\ 1/2 = 11/2 \times 7/2 = 77/4 = 19\ 1/4$

5. (A) If John gives 10 cards to Mary and 4 to Harry he has given 14 cards away. The remainder is $24 - 14 = 10$. If he sells the remainder for 5cents $10 \times 5 = 50$ cents.

6. (B) Get a common denominator: 1/2 + 2/3 = 1/2 = 3/6, 2/3 = 4/6. So 1/2 + 2/3 = 3/6 + 4/6 = 7/6 = 1 1/6.

7. (B) By reducing 25% to the fraction 1/4 we get, 25% of 160 = 1/4 × 160 = 40.

8. (C) Know what information to make use of. You want to find out how much Harry finally has. He starts with $15. He gives Mary $10 so he now has $5. Paul then gives Harry $2, so now Harry has $7.

9. (C) You would approximate 8.1 as 8 and 8.9 as 9. Then multiply 8 × 9 = 72.

10. (A) Try specific number like 3 and 5. 3 × 5 = 15. Add that to an even number, say 4, and you get 19, an odd number. However it may not always be even, so choose a different set of numbers. Say 7 and 11. You get 77, then add an even number, say 6. You get 83 an odd number. So I would venture that Choice A is correct.

In general you should know that an odd number times an odd number is odd and when an odd number is added to an even number you get an odd number.

11. (C) Write the number as N. So you get 2/3 × N = 6. Multiply both sides of the equality by 3 to get rid of the fraction. You get: 2 × N = 6 × 3. 2 × N = 18. Now divide by 2: You get N = 9.

12. (B) You have to realize that every complete rotation, that is 0 to 0, $4 comes out. So we divide $173 by 4 and we get 43 1/4. That means there was 43 complete revolutions and 1/4 left. Thus the hand must be point to the 1.

13. (C) You translate *is* to =, *what* to *x*, *of* to × (times) and *percent* to /100. 5 is what percent of 10 becomes

5 = x/100 × 10, or 5 = x/100 × 10. So, 5 = x (10/100); 5 = x/10 and so 50 = x.

14. (B) You write a proportion:

$$\frac{1 \text{ cup sugar}}{6 \text{ cups water}} = \frac{2 \ 1/2 \text{ cups sugar}}{x \text{ cups water}}$$

or

1/6 = 2 1/2/x

Cross multiply: x × 1 = 6 × 2 1/2 = 6 × 5/2

x = 15

15. (B) The area of the *shaded region* is found by subtracting the *area* of the *large circle* from the *area* of the *small circle*. Thus, the *area* of the *shaded region* is just 20 − 12 = 8 (Choice B).

16. (D) Label CD = 5 (since CD = BC) and ED = 8 (since ED = AE). This makes the perimeter 8 + 8 + 5 + 5 + 14 = 40 (Choice D).

17. What you want to know is what section of the graph looks as if it is 60% of the total graph (total cost). You can see that "Other Vegetables" make up a block that is about three fifths, or 60% of the total. All of the other sections make up less than one half (50 percent) of the total.

18. Translate words into math:

The contribution from Washington Junior High School was what part of the contributions from the other schools

25%   =   x   (20% + 15% + 40%)

25% = x (75%)

Divide both sides by 75 to get x alone:

25/75 = x

Reducing:

1/3 = x

19. Translate words into math:

Lincoln Junior High School made 20% of the total. 100% 5 $24,000 (given).

20% of   total =

$$\frac{20}{100} \times 24,000 = \frac{480,000}{100}$$

= 4,800

20. Translate words into math:

Call the number of boys b. Now translate:

The ratio of boys to girls is 3 to 4:

Note: 24 girls (given)

$$b/24 = 3/4$$

Multiply by 24 to get b alone:

$$b/24 \times 24 = 3/4 \times 24$$

$$b = 3/4 \times 24$$

Reduce:

$$b = 3/\cancel{4} \times \cancel{24}^{\,6}$$

$$b = 3 \times 6 = 18$$

Something you may want to note: Since it was stated that the ratio of boys to girls was 3 to 4, there must be fewer boys than girls. So there must be *less than 24* boys because there are 24 girls. You can therefore rule out Choices C and D immediately.

About the Author

Gary R. Gruber, PhD, is recognized nationally as the leading expert on the SAT, test-taking methods, and critical thinking skills. His books on test taking and critical thinking skills have sold more than seven million copies.